D0392497

PERSONAL FINANCE
S I M P L Y
UNDERSTOOD

PERSONAL FINANCE
—— S I M P L Y ——
UNDERSTOOD

PRUDENT STRATEGIES FOR SETTING AND ACHIEVING
FINANCIAL GOALS AND THE REASONS BEHIND THEM

C H R I S   S I M B E R

iUniverse LLC
Bloomington

PERSONAL FINANCE SIMPLY UNDERSTOOD
Prudent Strategies for Setting and Achieving Financial Goals and the Reasons behind Them

The information, ideas, and suggestions in this book are not intended to render professional advice. Before following any suggestions contained in this book, you should consult your personal accountant or other financial advisor. Neither the author nor the publisher shall be liable or responsible for any loss or damage allegedly arising as a consequence of your use or application of any information or suggestions in this book.

iUniverse books may be ordered through booksellers or by contacting:

iUniverse LLC
1663 Liberty Drive
Bloomington, IN 47403
www.iuniverse.com
1-800-Authors (1-800-288-4677)

Because of the dynamic nature of the Internet, any web addresses or links contained in this book may have changed since publication and may no longer be valid. The views expressed in this work are solely those of the author and do not necessarily reflect the views of the publisher, and the publisher hereby disclaims any responsibility for them.

Any people depicted in stock imagery provided by Thinkstock are models, and such images are being used for illustrative purposes only.
Certain stock imagery © Thinkstock.

ISBN: 978-1-4917-0521-6 (sc)
ISBN: 978-1-4917-0522-3 (hc)
ISBN: 978-1-4917-0523-0 (e)

Library of Congress Control Number: 2013916100

Printed in the United States of America

iUniverse rev. date: 10/03/2013

To my children, Sarah, Joshua, Thomas, and Jessica,
and with much thanks and love to my wife, Elaine, for
her contributions, patience, and encouragement.

Contents

List of Figures

Preface

Personal Finance Simply Understood began as a letter to my four adult children. We've had brief conversations over the years about different personal finance subjects, but there is so much more that I want them to understand and apply to their lives. Due to the amount of information and the need for examples, a one-on-one explanation would only scratch the surface, and they wouldn't be applying many of the principles right away. So I decided to simply write them a letter.

As I wrote and explained personal finance concepts, details, and methods and defined financial terms, the letter quickly grew in length. I covered the importance of managing personal finances and presented prudent strategies for setting and achieving financial goals, and then I added the reasoning behind the objectives and approaches along with examples. I also exposed the pitfalls and pointed out some of the wrong tendencies that have marked history and tend to be repeated over and over. At this point, it was obvious that the letter had become a book.

About ten years ago, while completing graduate work in finance, I began an in-depth study of personal finance, which continues today. My research included reading many books and papers on the subject, and I found specific insights and some valuable principles. But I haven't found an explanation of the basic areas of personal finance that everyone needs to understand, presented in a way that can be applied in our daily lives. I wanted to explain what needs to be done, why it needs to be done, why it's the right thing to do, and how doing it affects our financial situation.

While I was gleaning information and principles through research, I designed and developed a software application to manage my own financial information and to test various recommendations and calculations. As I tested various financial situations, the software helped to expose some financial concepts that seemed logical at first, but didn't provide a benefit when put into practice.

In 2012 when the software design and development were completed, I established Jazer Solutions to offer the software for sale as Jazer 100, a comprehensive personal finance management program (which is used for the analysis and calculations in this book). Even though the software provided a way to manage finances, the motivation to use it is another story. Understanding what needs to be done to manage our finances is only valuable if we understand its importance and we're motivated to do what needs to be done.

A few years ago as an associate professor at the Wesley J. Howe School of Business, I developed course material for some of the graduate courses that I was teaching. I applied that experience and some additional course development research to create scenarios and coursework for an academic version of the software. I used this version of the software to test financial scenarios for various simulated people and circumstances. Since these simulations covered a broad range of real-world financial situations for various age groups and situations, I incorporated this information when developing the personal finance examples in the book.

As the book neared completion, I wanted to share the information beyond my four children, and decided to publish *Personal Finance Simply Understood*.

Chris Simber

Introduction

Personal Finance Simply Understood will benefit anyone who would like to increase their understanding of personal finance, apply sound financial principles to better manage their money, set personal financial goals, and maintain a prudent course of action to meet those goals.

Personal finance encompasses everything in our lives that pertains to money and setting and achieving financial goals. We would expect some level of personal finance to be a part of our education, and yet we learn personal finance mostly from watching our parents and trial-and-error experiences (theirs and ours). It's not taught to a great extent in our school systems, and it isn't talked about much among friends and family. We're left on our own, for the most part, to get what we can from what we read, hear, and experience. Given this, we shouldn't be surprised that for many people, personal saving is an afterthought. They have trouble managing their finances and find out too late that they won't have enough saved to retire comfortably. Trial-and-error is often serving as the personal finance classroom.

In addition, the focus of the media and the majority of mainstream thinking today are contrary to sensible personal finance and achieving financial independence. We're bombarded with marketing that attempts to separate us from our money, and at the same time, we hear that we save too little and spend too much. Articles abound that tell us that we don't save enough and we won't have enough to retire comfortably, and most of those articles have a different idea of how much is enough and how much we should be saving weekly.

When I'm traveling and I come to place where I need directions, I need them from where I am at the time. If I call someone back home and they give me directions from where *they* are, it doesn't help me. Charting a course to financial independence is no different. Determining where we are financially and then setting a course toward where we want to be must be specific and personal, otherwise, it's not our plan, based on our information, and it has very little chance of succeeding.

The good news is that we can evaluate our financial situation ourselves and establish our own plans toward financial independence based on our financial information. *Personal Finance Simply Understood* provides the basis, mechanics, and reasoning behind the steps to accomplish this. In the following pages, we'll walk through personal finance, focusing on what we need to know and do and why, weighed against what we're seeing and hearing in the media.

This book is organized in a building-block format, and it is divided into sixteen chapters. In the first fifteen chapters you will learn:

- why we shouldn't do what everyone else is doing,
- how lifestyle choices affect our financial health,
- how to set achievable financial goals,
- why a budget is the foundation of personal finance,
- how spending habits are formed and persist,
- successful methods for debt elimination,
- why we need three savings plans,
- how to develop and implement savings plans,
- why it's possible to save large amounts of money,
- the basics of investing and investment types,
- the benefits of low-cost index funds,
- the benefits of diversification,
- how we establish an asset allocation strategy,
- how to develop a long-term savings strategy,
- how to build an investment portfolio step-by-step,
- how to plan for survivorship,

- how we determine our retirement savings amount,
- how we determine if our retirement savings will last through retirement, and
- how we determine how much life insurance is enough.

Each chapter contains examples to show how the methods and principles apply to financial information, including the calculations with explanations for relating personal information. The sample information used in the examples is consistent, whenever possible, to build on the previous concept or to compare the results of different methods. This highlights the benefits of the various approaches. Each chapter ends with a brief summary to reemphasize the primary ideas.

The sixteenth chapter is a summary of the steps toward financial independence, drawing on the primary concepts in the earlier chapters.

As far as the data is concerned, in some cases inflation rates, interest rates, and return-on-investment percentages and values are approximations or an average of composite data. In these instances, they are used to indicate a trend or for comparison with similar data and are not intended as actual rates or rates of return. In certain cases, rounding was applied to numerical values after calculations to simplify the example or explanation. The Vanguard mutual fund information is used with permission from The Vanguard Group and is noted where used. The financial planning, calculations, and analysis for *Personal Finance Simply Understood* were completed using Jazer 100 personal finance software from Jazer Solutions, LLC (www.jazersolutions.com). Unless otherwise indicated, the charts, tables, and graphs were produced using calculations, results, and tabular data from Jazer 100 or from estimates using historical trends. In other cases, sources are cited.

Admittedly, no single book could contain all of the information on all of the topics involved in personal finance, and I made decisions about how much material to include and how deep to explore each area based on what we all need to know. For instance, I explain what annuities are, how they work, and why we might want one, but there are hundreds of variations and provisions for annuities. I assumed that anyone considering an annuity would do some research and fully understand what they were purchasing before signing a contract. I noted these situations and added a comment when more information was recommended.

Personal financial management includes being cautious of trends and analyzing the big picture. This means not letting someone else do the work for us and just following their lead. We apply wise decision making and form a plan toward our goals based on sound knowledge and principles, diligently follow the plan, and review and adjust the plan as our lives change. It's pretty straightforward, not all that glamorous, and not terribly difficult ... and this is the good news.

Chapter One

Following the Herd

Even when we know something is wrong, if enough people say it is right we are inclined to change our opinion (or at least go along with the crowd). In fact, the more people giving the wrong answer, the less likely we are to go against the norm, especially if we're not absolutely sure. The opinion of the crowd can be a very strong influence, and it begins for most of us at a very young age. When we wanted to do what our friends were doing (even if it was wrong), many of us remember hearing our parents say, "If all your friends jumped off a bridge, would you jump too?" As we grew older, we saw the effects of peer pressure in our teens and later the benefits of following social and cultural norms in adulthood.

We have a strong tendency to be part of a group or to go with the flow, and in many cases it's a logical course of action. For example, if I hear enough people say that a restaurant is good, then I'm more apt to try it. It's impossible for me to know ahead of time, so I take their word for it. If it's not a good restaurant, well the damage is minimal. If people are saying the opposite and I choose not to go to the restaurant, again the damage is minimal. But in finances, the risks are much higher.

If a statistic says that most people are carrying $8,000 in credit card debt, do I feel good if I only have $3,000? Do I feel bad if my balances total $11,000? We're inclined to compare our circumstances to the average or the majority, and we tend to choose the opinion that puts our situation in the best light. With all of the contradicting views available, finding one that we like isn't all that difficult. And if the opinion is coming from someone famous or respected, well that's even better. In fact, the name of a group or the leader they're following can very often sway our opinion. We justify or rationalize by association.

The latest financial guru or a well-known financial magazine, newspaper, or website can influence savers and investors in a certain direction solely due to the popularity of the source. It could be the right direction or it could be a misguided opinion, but they've done the research and we don't have the time, so we follow the herd.

With so much information available and so many opinions, it's not surprising that we tend to settle on a few that we feel are reliable and let them do the thinking for us. Sifting through all the jargon and details can be overwhelming, so we look for someone famous or respected (or who agrees with us) and we follow along.

Another inclination to follow the herd comes from a feeling of being left out or of missing the boat. If our friends, family, acquaintances, or the media are talking about a new trend or opportunity, we wonder what it's all about and if we're missing out on something. For example, many individual investors make stock purchases based on information they hear at social gatherings. With all of the financial advice and recommendations available from experts in magazines, newsletters, and on television, they choose to listen to an acquaintance.

We should be aware of trends and opportunities, and we should also keep an eye on the herd and what they're doing, because we can get trampled (or caught up in it) if we're not careful. In the past, the herd has inflated stock prices by stampeding into specific areas and driving prices in parts of the market ridiculously high (or low).

This is what happened to housing prices starting in 2003 and it kept going for years as more and more people joined the crowd. In figure 1.1 below, the graph shows the average sales price for new homes over a twenty-year period. Notice the change on the graph beginning around 2003 as prices steadily increased. Now imagine if you had bought a home in 2006 at the peak of the price increase and what it would have been worth in January of 2009 after prices had fallen.

Figure 1.1   Average Sales Price of New Homes (20 Years)

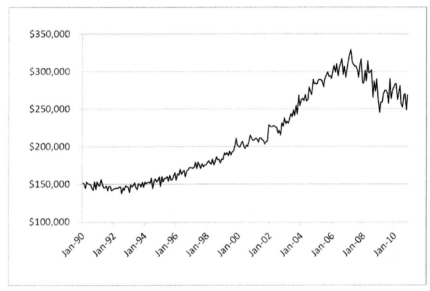

Data Source: US Census Bureau New Sales

As an example, let's say that I bought a home for $330,000 at the end of 2006 with a down payment of $40,000 and mortgaged $290,000 at 5 percent interest for thirty years

Home price 2006	$330,000
Down payment	$40,000
Mortgage	$290,000

In 2009, homes comparable to the one that I bought would be selling for about $248,000. This is $82,000 less than I paid for my house three years earlier and about $40,000 less than what I would still owe on the mortgage. If I had to sell the home, the list price would be less than I owed on the mortgage.

My mortgage balance in 2009	$276,091.71
Comparable home price 2009	$248,000.00

This situation affected many people and came as a shock to those who believed that real estate always appreciates in value. Historically it typically has, but home prices had been artificially inflated by a buying frenzy, and what occurred was the result of the herd mentality working together with the law of supply and demand.

The law of supply and demand in economics is a model of price determination (what the price of an item should be) based on the supply of a product in relation to the demand for the product. We see this at work throughout our economy. When there's an oil shortage, gas prices increase because the demand remains the same but the amount of gas available has decreased. When a new product comes out and everyone wants it (demand is high), the price tends to be high. Then as the demand decreases (less people are buying it), the price decreases.

Because of this relationship between supply, demand, and price, price can also be used to change the demand for a product through sale prices and store specials. Companies often lower the price of a product when supply is high to increase demand, and the increase in demand that results then lowers the supply.

When home prices began to increase in 2004, it was the result of an increase in demand for houses, which was driven by mortgage availability. Mortgages had become much easier to obtain because credit restrictions had been relaxed. Prior to this, banks required large down payments and closely scrutinized a buyer's ability to make the monthly mortgage payment. With looser restrictions, many more people could obtain a mortgage and buy a home. This created an increase in demand (more buyers) for houses that were on the market.

The increased demand was greater than the supply of homes that were for sale at the time, and this caused prices to rise. Soon buyers were offering to buy homes for more than the seller was asking to ensure that their offer would be accepted. In some cases, multiple buyers were bidding against each other for the same house, which caused prices to go even higher. People who had been considering moving saw their neighbors getting large amounts of money to sell their houses, and this prompted them to put their houses on the market too.

Other people saw an opportunity to make a large profit and listed their homes for sale at very high prices. Eventually, all of the homes that were being listed for sale were priced much higher than they would have normally been priced. *Why?* The listing price for a home is based on an appraisal that reflects recent sales of homes comparable in size and location. Since houses were selling for more, homes being listed for sale were priced higher as well.

This situation kept feeding on itself, and prices climbed steadily. Real estate agents were actually knocking on people's doors and offering to sell their homes for exceptional prices, and many homes were sold the day that they were listed for sale. Then the situation began to change as demand declined and the supply of homes on the market became greater than the demand.

Listed homes weren't selling as quickly, and people who needed to sell their homes had to lower prices in order to get interested buyers. Prices continued to fall as demand steadily decreased, and homes were now sitting on the market for longer periods of time without selling. This forced sellers to lower prices further.

At the same time, many people who had recently purchased homes at high prices weren't able to make their mortgage payments. Banks began to foreclose on the homes (take ownership of the property) and put these homes on the market at reduced prices in order to sell them quickly. (Banks don't like being in the real estate business.) Prices continued to fall until supply and demand finally evened out (reached equilibrium). At this point, prices for homes ended up about where they would have been without the wave.

If we take the home price data from figure 1.1 and draw a dotted line from the prebubble home prices to where they eventually settled (figure 1.2 below), we see approximately how the average sales price trend would have looked without the rise and fall.

Figure 1.2   Average Sales Price of New Homes (20 Years) — Trend

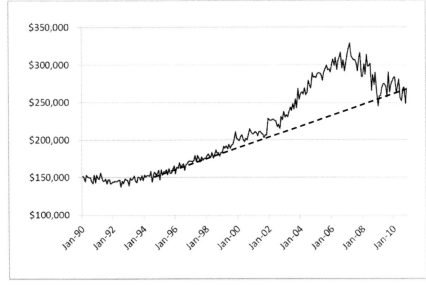

Data Source: US Census Bureau New Sales

It's interesting to note that the increase in the average sales prices of new homes from 1990 to 2000 was about 3.3 percent, and excluding the housing price bubble, the average increase from 2000 to 2010 was about 2.5 percent. In addition, existing home sales price increases averaged 3.4 percent annually from 1987 to 2009 (just slightly higher than new homes). The dotted line shows that if we remove the sales data from the period during the bubble, the average price for homes rises rather steadily at around 3 percent, which is fairly close to the average rate of inflation during that period. This would be considered acceptable, and we would expect housing prices to rise at or slightly above the rate of inflation. Looking at the graph now, we can easily see that something abnormal occurred. At the time, it wasn't as obvious, and unfortunately a lot of people were hurt financially.

Chapter Summary

The housing bubble is just one of many examples in history of a financial calamity caused or amplified by a herd mentality, and it is a glaring reminder for us to do the homework and think for ourselves. We should always step back and discern the noise and hype from good information and see how things fit into our financial plan. In many cases, the herd rushes into situations like this without taking the time to analyze the event and determine where it came from and where it might be headed. Remembering the financial trends of the past and the damage they caused can provide us with a healthy amount of skepticism when something new comes along.

Chapter Two

Lifestyle and Spending

The most important factor in managing our personal finances is our control over where our money is going. Before we establish financial goals or start out with a financial plan, we need to have a firm control of our spending habits, which are most often driven by our lifestyle decisions. For instance, I have to eat, but I don't need to eat at expensive restaurants twice a week. I need a car, but I don't need an expensive new car every two years. These are examples of lifestyle choices with financial consequences.

Whenever I think about lifestyle and personal finances, I'm reminded of the *The Millionaire Next Door: The Surprising Secrets of America's Wealthy* by Dr. Thomas J. Stanley, which analyzes the saving and buying habits of millionaires in America. We're conditioned by the media to think that wealthy people are driving around in the most expensive cars, living in the most expensive houses, and constantly traveling to exotic places. This is far from the truth, and as the book reveals, the secret to accumulating wealth and financial independence is simply consistent saving and living below our means.

We can't be out of debt and saving for our future needs if we're living beyond our means. It just doesn't work. When we make buying decisions, we should consider the influence that lifestyle has on the cost and discern between what we need and what we want. I might *need* a new coat, but I may *want* a very expensive coat from an expensive store. The material, quality, and how stylish it is (or how stylish the shop is where it's sold) are all factors that will determine the price. Let's consider two coats: an average coat that costs $70, and a very stylish coat that costs $230 from an expensive shop.

Average coat price (on sale)	$70
Stylish coat from an expensive shop	$230
Difference	$160

How we think and feel about the $160 difference in the price of the two coats will tell a lot about our shopping, spending, and saving habits. *Does the $160 difference matter?* An extra $160 on a debt payment would certainly have a positive impact, and $160 saved would earn interest, but I might really like the more expensive coat and like shopping in the upscale store.

A one-time decision to buy the more expensive choice might be fine, but typically our buying habits are consistent. Using the coat example above, consider the options below and the list of reasons for making the decision.

Shopping Decisions

- I'll buy the coat that I want because ...
    - I can afford it; it's only another $160.
    - I deserve it because I work hard.
    - I haven't bought myself anything lately.
    - I really, really, really like it.

- I'll keep shopping because ...
    - there's probably a similar coat that's less expensive.

- o   it's a stylish coat that will be out of style next year.
- o   that store is very expensive.

- • I'll put the purchase off because …
  - o   the same coat will cost much less in the off-season.
  - o   the coat that I have is fine; I can wait.
  - o   I would have to charge it, so I'll save to buy it later.

Impulse Buying

Sometimes we end up buying something when we were shopping for something else or not shopping at all. We're in a store or mall, and we see something, and the impulse strikes. If we let ourselves indulge in everything (or even most things) that we want, then the things that we need will have to wait, and most likely we will accumulate debt. What often happens is that our wants and impulsive spending crowd out our needs, and then later we're in trouble.

For instance, I need an emergency fund (which will be discussed later), and I need a car. If I choose a new car that will require a car loan, then I trade off saving that money in my emergency fund in order to make the car payments. I might even rationalize that I can sell the car if I hit hard times, so I buy the car. When a financial setback comes along (and it will), I look at my emergency fund and find that it's inadequate because I didn't save enough. Selling the car isn't an option because I need it to get to work, and I don't hold the title because of the loan. Now I'm stuck and I'll need to use credit to handle the setback.

We can't simply do away with an emergency fund or any other need because it suits us at the moment. We all have things that we want, and there's nothing wrong with wanting to have nice things. But if we simply want something, we should see it for what it is (a want and not a need) and keep it in the proper perspective. Needs should be taken care of first. Once we get spending under control and establish a saving plan, then we can consider wants with the proper perspective.

Simply Put, Don't Accumulate

Many of our drawers, closets, basements, attics, and garages contain a lot of stuff that at one time we thought we wanted or needed. It's amazing how quickly and how much stuff people can accumulate. This isn't practical or healthy, and having a lot of stuff around us clouds our thinking. The accumulation and storage of things that we don't use or need is wasteful, and if you visit a few yard sales one Saturday morning, you'll see a lot of items that were bought and never opened or were used only once or twice. Now these items are for sale at a huge discount.

If we ask ourselves before we buy something, "Do I really want it, and will I really use it?" most likely, we'll buy a lot less. Spur-of-the-moment and emotional purchases are very often regretted, and a lot of these items end up just being stored somewhere because we really didn't think before we bought them.

Price and Quality

When we're making a purchase, we should take our time, think about the level of quality we need, what we expect to pay, and where we should purchase the item. Then we can compare prices and stores and shop for a durable version of what we're buying.

Price should be one factor in our buying decisions, but the choice shouldn't be based on the lowest price or even the highest price. A lower-priced option may seem like a bargain, but the item may wear out very quickly. With the more expensive choices, there is a relationship between price and quality, but just because an item is the most expensive choice doesn't mean that it's the best choice. Very often the name brand or the name of the store where it's sold—and not the level of quality—is what made the item more expensive.

The Internet is great for researching the price, product ratings, and feedback on the quality of items before we buy. There are also companies that do product testing and report on the quality of products. It just takes us a little time to gather some information and compare, but it's time well spent.

Remembering a few general rules when shopping and asking ourselves a few questions can often reveal an unnecessary purchase before we spend. Listed below are some general rules and questions to consider when shopping.

Some General Rules for Purchases

- Think before you shop, and then think again before you buy.
    o Have I thought this over?
    o Is this a need or a want?
    o If it's a want, can I and should I afford it?
    o Will this just end up being stored somewhere?

- Shop around and buy quality products that are durable.
    o Is it made well and will it last?
    o Is there a guarantee or warranty?
    o Is the company reputable?
    o Will I be throwing this out in six months?

- Consider price, but not at the expense of quality.
    o Am I choosing this brand because it's the cheapest?
    o Am I paying more for a famous label?
    o Am I paying more because of the store name?

o   Am I paying more to have it now?

This might seem extreme, but forming good shopping habits has a direct impact on our financial health. All of the little amounts that we spend add up, and much of it is unnecessary if we think before we buy.

Chapter Summary

Before we establish financial goals or start out with a financial plan, we need to have a firm control of spending, and understanding our buying habits is a great place to start. Asking ourselves a few questions before a purchase can help with our shopping decisions, often change our minds about a purchase, and help us to see if we're buying driven by lifestyle or impulse. A minor change for the better can often have a major impact on our financial health.

Chapter Three

Financial Goals

When establishing financial goals, we assess the things that we need and want in life and associate a timeline and plan to achieve them. For some people, their financial goals are to someday be out of debt or have a better handle on their financial situation. But these types of goals don't lend themselves to an achievable plan, and progress can't be measured. Our financial goals need to be realistic, specific, and measurable. Instead of a goal to someday be out of debt, we establish a timeline such as having all of our credit card balances paid off in six months, or our car loan paid off in two years. With a timeline, we can develop a financial strategy to achieve the goal and measure our progress along the way.

Some of our goals will be short-term like saving for a vacation or car, and others will be longer term like owning a home or saving for retirement or a child's college fund. But they will each require a plan based on the cost and timeline. If my goal is to save $1,200 for a vacation that I'm going to take in four months, then I establish a plan to set aside $300 each month to achieve the goal.

$1,200 / 4 months = $300 monthly

If I'm unable to set aside $300 one month, then I'll need to increase the amount in the following month and keep track of my progress. Without a plan, there would be no way of knowing whether I'm on course to achieve the goal, and if I'm off course, by how much.

Our financial goals also need to be within (or better yet, below) our means of income and be a part of our spending plans. If we don't have control of our spending, then we haven't formed an achievable plan because it's left to chance. We may buy a lot of stuff that we want, but we'll be running as fast as we can to keep up with debt, which is a cycle that's very hard to break.

Setting Financial Goals

Each of our financial goals is unique because of our age, income, dependents, and other personal factors, but the basic structure and how we determine and set financial goals are common for all of us. We all have daily necessities, monthly bills, and the need to prepare for future events. The specific items associated with our goals might be somewhat different, but this is where we all begin. Below is a very simplified or foundational list of financial goals.

Simplified Financial Goals

- providing for everyday needs
- reducing/eliminating debt
- saving

First on the list of goals is providing for our everyday needs and necessities like food, sundries, shelter, and transportation. These weekly and monthly expenses make up the bulk of our budget and can't be ignored. If we had to, we could skip a deposit to our savings, but we can't decide not to buy food one month.

Next on the list is debt, which would include credit card balances and loans. These payments can't be skipped either. And last on the list is saving, which unfortunately tends to get the least attention.

If we take the simplified list above and add the specific items in each area, we see the framework for our financial goals. Below is an expanded list of financial goals with more specific items added.

Expanded Financial Goals

- Provide for everyday needs.
    - food and sundries
    - clothing
    - housing
    - car and transportation expenses

- Reduce/eliminate debt.
    - credit card balances
    - loans

- Saving
    - Save a small amount as a cushion.
        - unexpected bills like major car repairs
    - Establish savings for an emergency fund.
        - enough to pay for several months of expenses
    - Save for retirement.
        - long-term saving

Notice that the section for saving has been expanded into three separate items. The first is savings that is a cushion for unexpected expenses like major car repairs. The second is a rainy day account or emergency fund, and the last is a larger, long-term savings for when we retire or work in a reduced capacity later in life. These will be discussed at length in the chapters on saving.

Since we have to pay for necessities and make payments on debts, these items get the focus of our attention and affect all of our financial decisions. Saving gets the least of our attention because it is optional— or so it might seem.

If we continue to expand the "everyday needs" and "debt" lists above and include the amount of money associated with each item, we would have a complete list of where our money is going. This would essentially be our budget. Then when we include the amounts for our savings goals, we'll have a set of personal financial goals from which we can establish our complete financial plan.

Chapter Summary

All of our short- and long-term financial needs form the basis for our list of financial goals. As we establish our goals, they should be specific and have a timeline for achievement so that we can create a workable plan and measure our progress along the way. The financial plans that we develop should be based on our complete financial picture, which allows us to make adjustments more easily when they're needed.

Chapter Four

Budgets

The word *budget* tends to make a lot of people cringe because we tend to think of a budget as a constraint. A budget shouldn't be a list of what we *plan* to spend or a limit we're setting for ourselves. Our budget should be a list of where we actually spend our money and how much we really spend. If my budget is simply a plan that fits my income and doesn't reflect what I actually spend, then it really doesn't serve a purpose.

When we create a budget, we have to be realistic and come face-to-face with what we really spend. We can put it down on paper or use software, but we have to enter facts and not fiction or wishful thinking. Our checking account, bank, and credit card statements have the facts. This is where the money is really going. The needs, the wants, and what we shouldn't have spent all show up on these statements. This is why using our statements is a great way to create and maintain a budget. It forces us to review where the money is truly going and to use real costs in the process.

There are many available techniques for creating and maintaining budgets. For some people they work very well; for others, they work for a while; and for some, they don't work at all. Regardless of which method we use, the purpose is to pay regular attention to how much we make and spend and to actively manage our finances.

Reviewing a list of how we spend our money can be illuminating. Financial advisors are astounded by how many people have no idea where their money is going. They have income and a pretty good idea of their bills, but there's money missing somewhere, and they hope that the financial advisor can help them find it. Usually after compiling a complete list of monthly expenses (a budget) and answering some hard questions, the missing money is found. Below is a list of typical budget items to consider.

Sample Expenses

Personal	Utilities	Child Care	Charitable Donations
food	phone/cell phone	day care/sitter	place of worship
clothing	cable TV/Internet	baby supplies	charities
sundries	electric/gas/oil	diapers/formula	payroll deductions
necessities	water/sewer	allowance/clubs	local support
	trash service	child support	

Housing	Insurance	Installments	Leisure
mortgage	health	car payment 1	movies/sports events
property taxes	automobile	car payment 2	gifts/parties/holidays
association dues	home owners	credit cards	vacation/travel
rent	renters	personal loans	hobbies/crafts
maintenance	life	tax installments	gym/pool fees
		student loan	golf fees/country club

Transportation	Health Care	Education	Miscellaneous
fuel	medication	school tuition	lawn care
maintenance	office visits	registration	home security
tolls/parking	co-pay	books/supplies	tool maintenance
registration	dental	lab/service fees	dry cleaning/laundry
tags/inspection	optical	dues/clubs	work clothes/dues
bus fare	chiropractor	uniform/clothing	pet care/vet/meds

Once we have a complete list, we need to include the amount that we actually spend (not a budgeted amount) to each of the items. Segregating expenses into categories like the table below is also helpful.

Sample Budget

	Weekly	Monthly	Yearly
Living Expenses			
Food	$200.00	$866.67	$10,400.00
Sundries	$100.00	$433.33	$5,200.00
Phone	$20.77	$90.00	$1,080.00
Cable TV/Internet	$20.77	$90.00	$1,080.00
Housing Expenses			
Mortgage/rent	$600.00	$2,600.00	$31,200.00
Electric/gas	$69.23	$300.00	$3,600.00
Repairs/maintenance	$46.15	$200.00	$2,400.00
Water/sewer	$4.62	$20.00	$240.00
Auto Expenses			
Fuel	$60.00	$260.00	$3,120.00
Loan payment	$80.77	$350.00	$4,200.00
Auto insurance	$23.08	$100.00	$1,200.00
Maintenance	$23.08	$100.00	$1,200.00
Debt Reduction			
Credit card 1	$80.77	$350.00	$4,200.00
Credit card 2	$57.69	$250.00	$3,000.00
Credit card 3	$27.69	$120.00	$1,440.00
Credit card 4	$27.69	$120.00	$1,440.00
Total Expenses	$1,442.31	$6,250.00	$75,000.00

The category where items are listed isn't critical as long as every item is included. If you pay renters insurance or your own home-owners insurance, you might prefer to list them under housing. Just be sure that you capture all of the expenses and include them in weekly, monthly, and yearly amounts. Some expenses, like life insurance, are often paid quarterly, and we tend to forget about those and just handle them when they're due. This doesn't present an accurate picture of our expenses and can catch us off guard when the bill is due. If a bill is paid quarterly, which is typical of life insurance, divide the amount by three to arrive at a monthly expense amount. The same goes for water and sewer bills since they tend to be paid quarterly as well. Including these items often shows some expenses that we might be overlooking in our weekly and monthly lists.

The sample budget above segregates expenses into four major categories. I use a separate section for housing expenses and don't include them in the "living expenses" section to segregate the costs. We can use any number of categories that help us manage things. The expense amounts or costs are filled in depending on how they're paid. If a bill is paid monthly, then the weekly and annual amounts will need to be calculated.

One thing to watch for when making calculations, especially with income, is that we typically think of a month as four weeks, which isn't quite accurate. There are fifty-two weeks in a year and twelve months, so one month is actually more than four weeks.

52 weeks / 12 months = 4.33 weeks

Since I pay my $90 phone bill monthly, the weekly budgeted amount is not $90 / 4 weeks = $22.50. It's really $90 x 12 months / 52 weeks = $20.77.

This might seem trivial, but with larger amounts it makes a big difference as we'll see later. The "housing expenses" section includes an item for repairs and maintenance, which for me includes everything from a new garden hose to paint for the house trim. Like the other amounts, this should be typical of the amount that I spend and not an average. If I want any item to be a lower amount, then the reduction in spending comes before lowering the budgeted amount. If I simply reduce the amount budgeted and promise myself that I'll only spend up to the new budgeted amount, then I'm kidding myself. The reduction in spending comes first and then the reduction in the budget.

In the "auto expenses" section, I also include a maintenance item. This is often overlooked or brushed aside, and yet car maintenance costs can be very expensive. Be sure to review the suggestions for your budget and do a monthly review of the list and the amounts that you actually pay. We often forget significant items or fill in the wrong amount, but they'll eventually show up on one of our monthly statements.

After we have a listing of all expenses, the next item to consider is income. We always use our net income (take-home pay) for budgeting and analysis. In the sample budget, the total expenses were $1,442.31 weekly, $6,250 monthly, and $75,000 annually.

For an example, we'll assume a two-income couple who have $1,650 in combined weekly take-home pay as shown below.

Income Items

Income (net)	Weekly	Monthly	Yearly
Salary 1	$950	$5,200	$62,400
Salary 2	$700	$1,950	$23,400
Total net income	$1,650	$7,150	$85,800

Determining income for various periods is handled the same way as expenses. If we're paid weekly, we multiply by fifty-two to get an annual amount and then divide this by twelve to determine the monthly amount. Here's an example to show why I recommend this. If our weekly take-home pay is $500, multiplying by four results in $2,000 as a monthly income amount. Doing this omits four weeks of pay each year. If there were truly four weeks in each month, then a year would have forty-eight weeks. Using this calculation, annual income is $24,000.

Example 1 $500 Weekly Take-Home Pay

Weekly	$500.00	
Monthly estimate	**$2,000.00**	($500.00 x 4)
Annual estimate	**$24,000.00**	($2,000.00 x 12)

Let's re-calculate using the weekly take-home pay to determine the annual amount by multiplying by fifty-two weeks, and then we'll divide the annual amount by twelve to calculate the monthly amount.

Example 2 $500 Weekly Take-Home Pay

Weekly	$500.00	
Annual	**$26,000.00**	($500.00 x 52)
Monthly	**$2,166.67**	($26,000.00 / 12)

The difference between the monthly amounts is $166.67, and the annual income difference is $2,000. This is a large amount that could be overlooked. Saving the $166 difference each month for five years in a regular savings account would result in a $10,000 balance.

Now that we have established income, we subtract expenses from income to get what's called discretionary income (what's left over, or money not dedicated to any particular area). If we're spending more than we earn or expenses are greater than income, this number will be negative and will show us the amount of overspending each month.

In the example shown below, the amount is positive because there is some money ($900 monthly) that is not currently being applied to an area of the budget. This money is available for saving or debt reduction.

Discretionary Income

	Weekly	Monthly	Yearly
Total net income	$1,650.00	$7,150.00	$85,800.00
Total expenses	$1,442.31	$6,250.00	$75,000.00
Discretionary income	$207.69	$900.00	$10,800.00

If the expenses were greater than income, then we would need to make an adjustment by increasing our income, decreasing our spending, or both. Many people try to outrun expenses by constantly trying to increase their income. This can often work in the short term if we work additional hours or take on another job, but at some point we have to get control of expenses and live within (preferably below) our means. For many people, the more they make, the more they spend. So for them, controlling expenses is the only successful approach.

Since our example shows discretionary income available, we have several options. The money could be applied to debt by increasing a monthly payment amount, or it could be transferred to savings. Another option is to start a payroll deduction savings plan and save using direct deposit through our employer. This would lower our net income by transferring the amount directly to savings. If we direct the amount to an IRA, it could also have a positive impact on income taxes (covered later). In addition, if we're not donating to charity, this would be a great time to start. Giving has many positive results for us and for others and should be included in our financial planning.

It's also wise to review discretionary income and budgeted amounts frequently to be sure that any changes have been included. Some items may no longer be needed, or new items may need to be added from time to time. An accurate budget is the foundation that we build personal finance management on and use to establish plans for the future. To start an aggressive debt reduction plan or long-term savings plan, we'll need to be managing our monthly financial details. Since the goal is financial independence, spending some time to manage our finances is a small price to pay.

Checking Accounts

For many people, their checkbook is their budget. Deposits are made and bills are paid, and that's about it. Automatic payments, phone apps, and bank transfers simplify bill paying and at the same time eliminate a lot of visibility into what we're actually spending.

For instance, let's say that my gas and electric bill and my cell phone bill automatically charge one of my credit cards. I also have my cable and Internet bills paid directly from my checking account, and I use a debit card for groceries and a credit card for gas. When I pay my mortgage, I use a bank transfer. So I only have two credit card bills to pay and one transfer to make each month. I've scheduled the bills in my phone, and I get an alert that tells me when they're due. No matter where I am, when I get the alert, I can click and they're paid. This is very convenient, but I also tend to overdraw my account. I can see how much is in the account when I look at my account balance, but I don't know what has been paid, is pending, or is coming up. So in reality, I'm not managing the account; I'm simply using it.

To many of us, balancing our checking account is a headache we'd rather put off or even overlook. We even come up with tricks to keep things from getting out of hand like rounding up payments to the next dollar amount to accumulate an extra cushion in the account. But if we want to manage our finances, we have to be willing to put in the time, and this means reconciling balances at least once a month and double-checking expenses.

Reconciling or balancing our checkbook doesn't have to be a long, frustrating task. It really only takes a few minutes if we understand the bank statement cycle and balance the account each month. We also avoid having an overdrawn account, which could incur charges from our bank and a host of other inconveniences. Banks provide a lot of information online that we can access at any time, including our checking account transactions with the most recent transaction first. This gives us the ability to see the current state of the account as the bank sees it. Let's review the normal checking account cycle.

At the end of the monthly cycle, the bank makes our account statement available. This contains a summary section as well as details for all of the transactions and the account balances throughout the period. The account summary is a high-level view of the account for the month. It shows the beginning balance; the total amounts for deposits, checks, ATM and debit card transactions, fees, and other subtractions; and the balance for the end of the statement cycle. An account summary is shown below for a sample account that we'll use as an example.

Sample Account Summary

Account number	xxxx xxxx xxxx
Beginning balance on 07-26-13	$272.63
Deposits and other additions	$782.35
Checks posted	$323.98
ATM / debit card subtractions	$202.00
Other subtractions	$145.27
Ending balance on 08-27-13	$383.73

Most of us couldn't balance our checkbook using this information because the amounts have been combined into four categories, and there are probably transactions that we've made that aren't included. For instance, some transactions that were made late in the month may not have been received by the bank by the date of the statement. In this case, the statement was generated on August 27, and if I mailed a check on August 26, it would not have posted to the account at the bank, but I would have noted the amount in my checkbook ledger.

To review each item that is included in the summary information, we need to review the detailed list of transactions and compare those items with our checkbook ledger to balance the account. The detailed listing shows all of the transactions for the monthly period that the bank has processed. We'll use the detailed listing below as an example.

Sample Account Detailed List of Transactions

Date Posted	Amount ($)	Resulting Balance ($)	Transaction
07-27	782.35+	1054.98	Deposit
07-30	200.00-	854.98	Check 123
08-03	145.27-	709.71	Store card Des: check pmt. #124
08-12	123.98-	585.73	Check 125
08-15	200.00-	385.73	ATM transaction
08-15	2.00-	383.73	ATM withdrawal fee

The first transaction above is a deposit of $782.35. From the account summary above, we know that the beginning balance for the month from the bank's point of view was $272.63. Adding the deposit of $782.35 to the starting balance of $272.63 gives us $1054.98, which agrees with the "resulting balance" column above.

The next three items on the list are checks. Notice the different way that check 124 (posted on August 3) is shown. Checks often appear differently depending on how they're processed by the bank, and the information isn't always obvious. If we total the three checks, we get a number that is different from the amount for "checks posted" on the account summary.

Sample Account Summary:
Checks posted: $323.98

Sample Account Detailed List of Transactions
Total of checks: $200.00 + $145.27 + $123.98 = $469.25

The difference in the amounts has to do with the way that the bank handled check 124. If we remove check 124 from our addition, the total agrees with the account summary amount for "checks posted": $200.00 + $123.98 = $323.98.

We can also see that $145.27, which is the amount for check 124, is listed in the account summary under "other subtractions." It was handled by the bank, but not the same way that a normal check would be posted. This agrees with information on the statement in the "checks posted in numerical order" section of the statement that the bank provides (shown below). Check 125 has an asterisk next to the number indicating a gap in check numbers because check 124 is missing. Again, it was handled by the bank, but not as a normal check posting. This can be confusing and is often overlooked.

Checks Posted in Numerical Order

Check #	Posting date	Amount
123	07-30	$200.00
125*	08-12	$123.98

Our simple example had very few transactions. When a full month of normal account activity is reviewed, there can be multiple cases where the way transactions are handled and the timing of postings can make the statement balance and our checkbook balance amounts very different.

Next, we'll walk through the checkbook ledger for the example and compare it to the information that the bank provided. Our ledger should be updated with all of our transactions as we make them or as soon as possible thereafter. This is an area where many people have difficulty, and it adds to the work involved to balance the ledger with the account.

The ledger will tend to be different from the bank statement because of the timing of bank processing, but this is resolved by reconciling the account and ledger regularly. The ledger for the example is shown below.

Sample Checkbook Ledger

Number, code	Date	Transaction description	Payment, fee withdrawal (-)	Deposit credit (+)	
					$272.63
					-200.00
123	07/24	Heat and elec.	200.00		72.63
					782.35
AD	07/27	Automatic deposit		782.35	854.98
					-145.27
124	07/29	MyStore credit card	145.27		709.71
					-123.98
125	08/05	MyMechanic garage	123.98		585.73
					-202.00
ATM	08/15	ATM withdrawal	202.00		383.73
					-30.00
126	08/17	Nephew's b'day	30.00		353.73
					-150.00
127	08/25	Credit card pmt	150.00		203.73
					782.35
AD	08/28	Automatic deposit		782.35	986.08

The first transaction is check 123. The date of the transaction and description have been entered, along with the amount in the "payment, fee, withdrawal (-)" column. The next transaction (labeled "AD" at the far left) is an automatic deposit. This is an automatically deposited paycheck. The date of the transaction and a description have been entered, and $782.35 is noted in the column labeled "deposit, credit (+)." Using the proper column helps with the accuracy of the balance as amounts go in and out of the account and for quickly finding errors.

The next two entries are checks 124 and 125, including the dates of the transactions and descriptions along with the amounts in the "payment, fee, withdrawal (-)" column. The next transaction is the

ATM withdrawal including the $2.00 ATM fee added to the amount to ensure that it isn't forgotten. ATM transaction fees tend to be forgotten until they show up on the statement, and this complicates balancing the account because ATM charges are small amounts. When they're overlooked, they have to be located on the bank statement under the section for "detailed list of transactions" and noted on our ledger after the fact. This adds unnecessary work that can be avoided by including it in the ledger when the transaction is made.

Next there are two more checks, 126 and 127, and the last entry is another automatic deposit. We reconcile the statement and the ledger by matching the transactions. The list of transactions from the bank statement is repeated below for convenience.

Sample Account Detailed List of Transactions

Date Posted	Amount ($)	Resulting Balance ($)	Transaction
07-27	782.35+	1054.98	Deposit
07-30	200.00-	854.98	Check 123
08-03	145.27-	709.71	Store card Des: check pmt. #124
08-12	123.98-	585.73	Check 125
08-15	200.00-	385.73	ATM transaction
08-15	2.00-	383.73	ATM withdrawal fee

Sample Checkbook Ledger (partial)

Number, code	Date	Transaction Description	Payment, fee withdrawal (-)	Deposit credit (+)	
					$272.63
					-200.00
123	7/24	Heat and elec.	200.00		72.63
					782.35
AD	7/27	Automatic deposit		782.35	854.98

The automatic deposit transaction on the bank statement is actually the second entry in the ledger. Although check number 123 was written on July 24, it wasn't posted by the bank until July 30. After taking both transactions into account, the statement and ledger balances agree up to this point. It's a good idea to check off each transaction in the ledger as shown below as it's located on the statement. Doing so helps to keep track of the items that have been reconciled. This also notes in the ledger, for future reference, that the bank processed the transaction.

The next two checks and the ATM transaction that appear on the statement are checked off on the ledger, and the balances are compared. The statement and ledger have been reconciled up to this point, and the balances agree. On the line in the ledger where the account has balanced, it's a good idea to make a note. This way, if we can't reconcile the statement and ledger in the future, at least we know that the problem must be somewhere after the point where they last balanced.

Sample Checkbook Ledger

Number, code	Date	Transaction Description	Payment, fee Withdrawal (-)	Deposit Credit (+)	$272.63
					-200.00
123	7/24	Heat and elec.	200.00	√	72.63
					782.35
AD	7/27	Automatic deposit		√ 782.35	854.98
					-145.27
124	7/29	MyStore credit card	145.27	√	709.71
					-123.98
125	8/05	MyMechanic garage	123.98	√	585.73
					-202.00
ATM	8/15	ATM withdrawal	202.00	√ BALANCED	383.73
					-30.00
126	8/17	Nephew's b'day	30.00		353.73
					-150.00
127	8/25	Credit card pmt.	150.00		203.73
					782.35
AD	8/28	Automatic deposit		782.35	986.08

When the next statement is available or we log in to the account online, we can continue balancing the ledger and the account with check 126 and go on from there. The key is to balance the account regularly so that there is less chance of error, and we're not reviewing a long list of transactions. Reconciling them frequently takes less time and makes finding errors a lot easier.

Chapter Summary

Effectively managing our finances requires an established baseline of financial information (budget) and a commitment to frequently review transactions to be sure that we're capturing accurate information. With a budget in place, we can monitor our discretionary income and use it to our benefit by paying down debt or increasing savings. Frequently balancing checking and debit accounts makes the task much easier and ensures that we're aware of our cash-flow situation.

Chapter Five

Debt

Debt can be overwhelming and burden us in a way that affects every aspect of our lives, including our health. In fact, the emotional, psychological, and physical effects of debt are starting to get increased attention from the medical community. If we take on debt and fail to manage it, debt can easily get to the point where it manages us and affects all of our financial decisions.

The sources of debt accumulation are not a secret. We buy things that we can't afford and use borrowed money to do it. Sometimes necessity and circumstance give us no other choice, but generally speaking, we spend money that we don't have rather than wait and save. We see something, we want it now, and we don't have the cash — so we buy it on credit. We rationalize that we can (or will be able to) afford it and that we'll figure out how to pay for it.

It's no help that advertisers and the media encourage this kind of spending with ads that tell us that we deserve it, we'll regret not having it, or it will impress our friends. Ads like this are everywhere for one reason: they work, and they work really well. When we see or hear this type of ad, we need to remind ourselves that it has been worded in a way to separate us from some of our money. Before we act, we need to consider whether spending the money is part of our financial goals.

Simply Put, Don't Accumulate Debt

People buy a lot of things that they don't need, and in some cases don't even want, and they often buy them with credit. It's interesting that people who use cash spend less on average than people using debit or credit cards. Apparently we're less likely to buy when we see the money that we're spending, as opposed to just swiping a plastic card. But credit card offers fill our mailboxes on a regular basis, and stores offer us discounts if we sign up for (and use) their credit card on the spot. The use of credit has reached a critical point for a lot of people, and at the same time it's becoming an acceptable way to buy almost everything.

Credit also allows us to stretch out the payments over time, making things seem more affordable. Maybe I can't afford $500 today, but I can afford $50 a month for ten months. Car dealers rely on this thinking. They don't ask us how much we want to spend on a car; they ask how much of a monthly payment we can afford. The idea is to get us to think about the monthly payment and to get our attention away from the price and the fact that we'll be paying for a long time. We don't consider the total cost. Here's an example using an $18,000 car which actually costs $21,131.44.

Price of the Car: $18,000   Amount Financed: $18,000

Monthly Payment	Length of Loan	Interest Rate	Total Interest Paid on Loan	Total Cost of Car
$352.19	60 months	6.5%	$3,131.44	$21,131.44

The loan adds $3,131.44 in interest to the price paid for the car and impacts our monthly budget by $352.19 for five years. This is interest over time, working against us.

To see the effect of time, we'll shorten the duration of the loan to three years (shown below). The monthly payment will be larger by $200, but the total amount of interest paid on the loan is lowered to $1,860.56, which is $1,270.88 less.

Price of the Car: $18,000   Amount Financed: $18,000

Monthly Payment	Length of Loan	Interest Rate	Total Interest Paid on Loan	Total Cost of Car
$551.68	**36 months**	6.5%	**$1,860.56**	**$19,860.56**

There is always a price when we borrow (use someone else's money), except on those rare occasions when we can borrow at zero percent interest. As we just saw, shortening the duration of a loan reduces the amount of interest paid, but if we can pay half of the price for the car in cash, again the "total interest" and "total cost of the car" amounts will be lower as shown below.

Price of the Car: $18,000   Amount Financed: **$9,000**

Monthly Payment	Length of Loan	Interest Rate	Total Interest Paid on Loan	Total Cost of Car
$275.84	36 months	6.5%	$930.28	$18,930.28

There are three variables at work here: the loan amount, the term (length) of the loan, and the interest rate (which we'll look at later). Changing any of these will change the total amount that we pay and the monthly payment.

Credit cards work the same way, except the duration or term of the loan is determined by our balance and our payment habits. We're not borrowing for a specific length of time with a credit card unless we make the minimum payment. If we pay the balance in full, then the term of the loan is zero months, and there is no interest paid.

The problem with credit cards occurs when we don't pay the full amount each month. In fact, many people pay the minimum payment amount. In either case, the balance and interest rate become very important. When credit cards were first introduced, the interest paid on the balance was tax deductible, and the interest rate being charged wasn't as important. This was done as an incentive for people to use credit. A few years later when using credit cards had become widespread, the tax deduction was stopped. Suddenly, the interest rate became much more important.

To show the effects of payment habits, the table below shows three scenarios using the same credit card balance of $650 with an interest rate of 12 percent, but using different monthly payments. Changing the monthly payment changes how long it will take to pay off the balance (term in months) and the total interest that will be paid.

Credit Card Balance: $650   Interest Rate: 12%

Monthly Payment	Term in Months	Total Interest Paid	Total Amount Paid
$25.19	30 months	$105.59	$755.59
$221.01	3 months	$13.04	$663.04
$650.00	0 months	$0.00	$650.00

Credit card companies now include on their monthly statements the length of time that it would take to pay off the balance and the total amount paid if we choose to make the minimum payment. In the table above, the first row shows the results of making the minimum payment for this example.

The example above assumes that this credit card is not being used to make purchases. The balance is reduced as a result of the payment and interest. When we continue to use a card with a balance, the balance and the interest paid are affected by our monthly charges.

Consider if we only made the minimum payment of $25.19 and typically charged another $100 each month to this card. Since the payment is less than we're charging each month, we know where this is headed.

We would be paying $25.19 each month, but the payment would only lower the balance by just $18.69 (the payment of $25.19 minus the interest charge of $6.50), and the balance would increase as a result of the $100 in additional purchases. As shown below, this is a recipe for problems since the balance just keeps growing.

Credit Card Minimum Payment

Starting balance	$650.00
Portion of payment applied to the balance	$18.69*
Monthly charges	$100.00
New balance	$731.31

* $25.19 payment - $6.50 interest = $18.69

One way to keep ourselves from getting into this situation is to understand the causes. Credit card debt is often caused by impulse buying, so if we can wait a day and sleep on a purchase, especially one that involves credit, we usually won't make the purchase. We come to our senses and realize that we don't really need it, that we can make do nicely with what we already have, or that the desire to have it is outweighed by the cost and additional debt.

This is one reason why car dealers want a deposit before we leave the showroom. They know how this works, and they want us to make the commitment to buy and not think about it for a day or two. Whenever we feel pressured to buy something, that's a signal for us to stop and think about it for a day or two. Very often we'll be glad we didn't make the purchase.

Another cause of overspending and incurring debt is impractical reasoning. If I'm going on a ski trip, and I've never skied before, should I spend hundreds of dollars on personal ski equipment or rent when I get there? I could rationalize buying the equipment by telling myself that the rented equipment won't fit quite right, and I should have my own. Or maybe I want to look like I know what I'm doing even though I've never been on skis before. This is impractical reasoning.

Another example is a spur-of-the-moment vacation when I'm under a lot of stress and I think that a vacation will make me relax and feel better. I can go online and use my credit card to charge a nice vacation package, and I get away. A vacation taken on credit could be long forgotten before the debt is paid, so I've actually added to my stress.

A shopping spree because we're bored or an expensive indulgence because we've been working hard are impractical uses of credit and will add to our debt burden. If an ad tells us to do something nice for ourselves or that we deserve it, we shouldn't think that they're really thinking about us.

There are practical reasons for using a credit card, but we have to consider the cost and be sure to only buy using a credit card when we have the money available. That way we can pay the balance in full when the bill is due. With loans, we need to be sure that we understand the total amount we'll be paying with interest, and we should consider our ability to make the payments over the full term of the loan. We should always ask ourselves if we really want to borrow the money. In many cases, waiting and saving for the purchase is a wise choice. When we think that we can't wait, we should remember that we've gone this long without it and have done just fine.

Too Late

If we have debt accumulated, there are several debt-reduction approaches worth considering. We can focus on a specific area of debt, like paying the largest debt first, or use debt consolidation and simplify things with a single bill. If we want to focus on a specific area of debt, there are three methods typically used. We can concentrate on paying the smallest debt, the largest debt, or the debt with the highest interest rate. Each of these methods has a different benefit and can be successful depending on our situation.

Let's walk through an example to see the effects of these different approaches. For comparison, we'll begin with the same four debts and balances as shown below. There is a car loan, and there are three credit card balances. The columns list the interest rates, payment that is being applied, the current balance, and then the forecasted balances for six months using the payment applied and interest rate.

The total debt balance that we're starting with is $11,950, and there is $650 available each month for the debt payments. Each approach will apply the $650 in different ways to reduce the total debt.

Example: Payment Plan

Debt Title	Rate	Payment	Balance	Jan-13	Feb-13	Mar-13	Apr-13	May-13	Jun-13
Car loan	7%	$200.00	$8,000.00	$7,846.67	$7,692.44	$7,537.31	$7,381.28	$7,224.34	$7,066.48
Credit card 1	12%	$250.00	$2,600.00	$2,376.00	$2,149.76	$1,921.26	$1,690.47	$1,457.37	$1,221.95
Credit card 2	15%	$100.00	$450.00	$355.63	$260.07	$163.32	$65.36	$0.00	$0.00
Credit card 3	11%	$100.00	$900.00	$808.25	$715.66	$622.22	$527.92	$432.76	$336.73
Total		$650.00	$11,950.00	$11,386.54	$10,817.93	$10,244.11	$9,665.03	$9,114.47	$8,625.16

Paying the Largest Debt First

The largest debt in the example is the car loan. Since we have a limited amount to apply to debt each month, we can only increase the car payment amount by reducing the payments for the credit cards. We'll reduce each of them by $50, which will free up $150 to add to the $200 car loan payment.

Note: If you consider this approach, be sure that your loan allows you to increase the payment amount, and that early payoff is accepted. With some loans, there is actually a penalty for paying the loan balance off ahead of schedule.

In the table below, the car payment amount has been increased from $200 to $350, and the credit card payments have been lowered by $50 each.

Example Payment Plan—Largest Debt First

Debt Title	Rate	Payment	Balance	Jan-13	Feb-13	Mar-13	Apr-13	May-13	Jun-13
Car loan	7%	$350.00	$8,000.00	$7,696.67	$7,391.56	$7,084.68	$6,776.01	$6,465.54	$6,153.25
Credit card 1	12%	$200.00	$2,600.00	$2,426.00	$2,250.26	$2,072.76	$1,893.49	$1,712.43	$1,529.55
Credit card 2	15%	$50.00	$450.00	$405.63	$360.70	$315.20	$269.14	$222.51	$175.29
Credit card 3	11%	$50.00	$900.00	$858.25	$816.12	$773.60	$730.69	$687.39	$643.69
Total		$650.00	$11,950.00	$11,386.54	$10,818.64	$10,246.25	$9,669.33	$9,087.86	$8,501.78

Looking across the months above, the car loan balance is now reduced much faster, and the credit card balances are stretched out further. Also, notice the total debt across the bottom row compared to the original table. The total debt is actually higher at first than the original plan, and then we begin to see the benefits in May. The total debt is reduced faster because we're lowering the car loan balance, which eliminates interest charges on a very large debt. This allows more of the payment each month to be applied to the debt balance instead of going to interest. Each month, the interest that we pay on debt works against our financial plans.

Using this method, when the car loan balance is paid off, we would concentrate on the next largest debt (credit card 1) by adding the full amount that was being paid on the car loan. This would increase the payment for credit card 1 to $550, which would pay off the balance very quickly. Once the balance on credit card 1 has been eliminated, the amount from that payment would be added to the payment for credit card 3, which is the next largest debt. This continues until all debts have been eliminated.

This method has the benefit of reducing a large debt and the interest that applies to a large debt, but it also takes longer than the other methods. Even with the increased payment, it will take over two years to pay off the car loan. Meanwhile, we would be paying interest on the credit card debts.

Paying the Smallest Debt First

This method tends to be a favorite because small debts can be eliminated fairly quickly. In the example, the smallest debt is credit card 2, and we'll use a similar approach as before. The car loan payment must be at least $200, so we'll just be taking $50 from the original payment amounts for credit cards 1 and 3. The payment for credit card 2 will now be $200, and with this payment amount, the balance is eliminated in March as shown below.

Example Payment Plan—Smallest Debt First (Step 1)

Debt Title	Rate	Payment	Balance	Jan-13	Feb-13	Mar-13
Car loan	7%	$200.00	$8,000.00	$7,846.67	$7,692.44	$7,537.31
Credit card 1	12%	$200.00	$2,600.00	$2,426.00	$2,250.26	$2,072.76
Credit card 2	15%	$200.00	$450.00	$255.63	$58.82	$0.00
Credit card 3	11%	$50.00	$900.00	$858.25	$816.12	$773.60
Total		$650.00	$11,950.00	$11,386.54	$10,817.64	$10,383.67

With the balance on credit card 2 eliminated, the amount from that payment is added to the payment for credit card 3, which is the next lowest balance (shown below). Credit card 3's payment will become $250 starting in April, and the balance on that card will be eliminated by July.

Example Payment Plan— Smallest Debt First (Step 2)

Debt Title	Rate	Payment	Balance	Apr-13	May-13	Jun-13	Jul-13
Car loan	7%	$200.00	$7,537.31	$7,381.28	$7,224.34	$7,066.48	$6,907.70
Credit card 1	12%	$200.00	$2,072.76	$1,893.49	$1,712.42	$1,529.55	$1,344.84
Credit card 2	15%	$0.00	$0.00	$0.00	$0.00	$0.00	$0.00
Credit card 3	11%	$250.00	$773.60	$530.69	$285.56	$38.17	$0.00
Total		$650.00	$10,383.67	$9,805.46	$9,222.31	$8,634.20	$8,252.54

In August after credit card 3 is paid off, the $250 payment would be added to credit card 1, which increases that payment to $450, and the balance is paid off in just three months (shown below).

Example Payment Plan— Smallest Debt First (Step 3)

Debt Title	Rate	Payment	Balance	Aug-13	Sep-13	Oct-13	Nov-13
Car loan	7%	$200.00	$6,907.70	$6,747.99	$6,587.36	$6,425.78	$6,263.27
Credit card 1	12%	$450.00	$1,344.84	$908.29	$467.37	$22.05	$0.00
Credit card 2	15%	$0.00	$0.00	$0.00	$0.00	$0.00	$0.00
Credit card 3	11%	$0.00	$0.00	$0.00	$0.00	$0.00	$0.00
Total		$650.00	$8,252.54	$7,656.28	$7,054.73	$6,447.83	$6,263.27

When the balance for credit card 1 is paid off in November, the $450 is then applied to the car loan (if permitted).

Example Payment Plan— Smallest Debt First (Step 4)

Debt Title	Int. Rate	Payment	Balance	Dec-13	Jan-14	Feb-14	Mar-14
Car Loan	7%	$650.00	$6,263.27	$5,649.81	$5,032.76	$4,412.12	$3,787.86
Credit Card #1	12%	$0.00	$0.00	$0.00	$0.00	$0.00	$0.00
Credit Card #2	15%	$0.00	$0.00	$0.00	$0.00	$0.00	$0.00
Credit Card #3	11%	$0.00	$0.00	$0.00	$0.00	$0.00	$0.00
Total		$650.00	$6,263.27	$5,649.81	$5,032.76	$4,412.12	$3,787.86

Paying the smallest debt first gives us some momentum quickly and incentive to keep going. With this method, all of the credit card debt was eliminated in eleven months. Of course, our ability to do this depends on controlling our spending and not adding any new debt.

Paying the Debt with the Highest Interest Rate First

If we decided to pay down the debt with the highest interest first, we would increase the payment on credit card 2 (which also happens to be the smallest debt). When that balance was paid off, we would add that payment to credit card 1. When that balance was paid off, we would concentrate on credit card 3, and after that we would concentrate on the car loan. If you're being plagued by high interest rates, this may be the preferred approach. There are people who are paying interest rates near 24 percent on credit card balances. For them, this method might be worth considering, especially if there is a high balance on the account.

Comparing the Methods

The table below shows the approximate time to pay off all of the balances in the example using the three debt elimination methods. For the comparison, it was assumed that no additional charges were made to the credit cards.

Debt Elimination Method Comparison

Method	Time to Eliminate Debt
Largest debt first	25 months
Smallest debt first	18 months
Debt with the highest interest rate first	20 months

Debt Consolidation

With debt consolidation, all of our debts are combined into a single payment. It usually involves a separate loan for the total amount of our debt, and the money from the loan is used to pay off all other debts.

Our other debt balances are paid off, and we have one large payment to make on the new debt.

Sometimes this is handled through a third party that we pay a single amount to each month, and they in turn pay the companies that we owe. The third party charges a fee for handling this process. The additional fees are often added to the interest charged, so we need to thoroughly understand the costs with this approach.

I'm not fond of the debt consolidation method because it's more of a convenience approach and requires a great deal of discipline to succeed. Once all of the previous debt balances are removed, people often continue to charge and accumulate more debt. The situation in the end is worse than it was in the beginning, and the root of the problem wasn't addressed.

Debt Reduction Summary

Any of the debt reduction methods can be used successfully to eliminate debt. Personally I prefer paying off the smallest debt first because of the momentum it builds quickly. If you use one of these approaches, form a plan, review the plan often, and keep very close track of your progress. Seeing the progress you're making is a great incentive to continue and even increase the payment amounts and retire the debts sooner.

The key is to keep spending under control while working a debt reduction plan and eventually eliminate all debt. We would all prefer to carry no debt, but for most of us, the reality is quite different. Like every other obstacle in life, how we face it and act on our options is what matters.

Mortgages

Buying a home is a major event in our lives, and the excitement can easily overshadow the long-term financial commitment we're about to make, especially when we've found a home that we love. The property taxes, maintenance, and mortgage obligation that we're taking on seem to take a backseat to the excitement. We tend to see a mortgage much like a car loan and focus on the monthly payment, while overlooking the cost of the loan or total amount of interest that will be paid over the life of the mortgage. We'll look at several situations in this section and review different ways that mortgage payments and costs can be reduced.

There are several different kinds of mortgages. The most popular are fixed rate (the interest rate never changes) and ARMs or adjustable rate mortgages (the interest rate fluctuates according to a set criteria). There are also interest-only mortgages (the payment is only interest, the loan is never paid off) and graduated and balloon payment mortgages (the payments rise over time).

One of the greatest costs associated with a mortgage is interest. In the case of a mortgage with a changing interest rate, we can't calculate the total amount of interest that will be paid. For a fixed rate mortgage, we know the interest amount will always be the same, so we can calculate the interest over the entire period of the loan. This will allow us to make certain changes to the mortgage in our examples to see the effects. The interest rate and the duration of the mortgage have the greatest impact on the monthly payment and total interest amount, so we'll look at them individually.

As an example, we'll assume that we're buying a house with a $275,000 purchase price. Our down payment will be $25,000, so we'll be financing $250,000 through a fixed rate mortgage. We'll assume that the loan is for thirty years, which is the standard mortgage duration, and we'll review the effects of different interest rates.

Home price	$275,000
Down payment	$25,000
Mortgage amount	$250,000

The table below shows the monthly payment, total interest paid over the life of the mortgage, and the total payback amount. Notice the "total payback amount" column to the right and how the numbers compare to the amount we're borrowing. In the "total interest paid" column, we see the cost of the loan. At a 6 percent interest rate (bottom row), the total interest paid is more than the mortgage amount and higher than the original price of the house. This should get our attention.

Mortgage of $250,000, for 30 Years, at Different Interest Rates

Interest Rate	Monthly Payment	Total Interest Paid	Total Payback Amount
3.5%	$1,122.61	$154,140.23	$404,140.23
4.0%	$1,193.54	$179,673.78	$429,673.78
4.5%	$1,266.71	$206,016.77	$456,016.77
5.0%	$1,342.05	$233,139.44	$483,139.44
5.5%	$1,419.47	$261,010.10	$511,010.10
6.0%	$1,498.88	$289,595.48	$539,595.48

Mortgage Duration

Next, we'll look at the effect of changing the mortgage duration or number of years that we'll be paying the loan. The most popular durations for mortgages are fifteen and thirty years. The table below shows the change in the monthly payment and total interest paid as the time period for the loan changes.

The monthly payment decreases as the duration increases, and this tends to make people more comfortable with the mortgage. They don't always consider the significant increase in interest that will be paid over the life of the loan.

Mortgage of $250,000, at 4.5% Interest, over Different Time Periods

Time Period	Monthly Payment	Total Interest Paid	Total Payback Amount
15 year	$1,912.48	$94,246.98	$344,246.98
20 year	$1,581.62	$129,589.62	$379,589.62
25 year	$1,389.58	$166,874.36	$416,874.36
30 year	$1,266.71	$206,016.79	$456,016.79

To highlight the differences, let's compare just the fifteen-year and thirty-year mortgages, since they're the most popular (shown below). The monthly payment for the fifteen-year mortgage is $645.77 higher, but the total interest paid is $111,769.81 lower. There are also 180 fewer payments to make since it will be paid off in fifteen years. Remember, the principal (amount we borrowed) is the same ($250,000) in both cases. The difference is the amount of interest that will be paid.

Comparison: 15-Year and 30-Year Mortgage

Time Period	Monthly Payment	Total Interest Paid	Total Payback Amount
15 year	$1,912.48	$94,246.98	$344,246.98
30 year	$1,266.71	$206,016.79	$456,016.79
Difference	$645.77	$111,769.81	$111,769.81

For the example so far, we have used the same mortgage amount, but as we saw in the car loan example earlier, we can save money in interest by lowering the amount that we borrow. To do this, we would need to increase the down payment on the house.

Again, we're buying a $275,000 house with a thirty-year mortgage at 4.5 percent interest. The table below shows the effects of increasing the down payment to lower the mortgaged amount. Comparing the first two rows in the table, by increasing the down payment from $25,000 to $50,000, we lower the monthly payment by $126.67 and lower the total amount of interest paid by $20,601.71.

Effects of Increasing the Down Payment Amount, 30-Year Mortgage

Down Payment	Mortgage Amount	Monthly Payment	Total Interest Paid	Total Cost of the House
$25,000	$250,000	$1,266.71	$206,016.79	$456,016.71
$50,000	$225,000	$1,140.04	$185,415.08	$460,415.08
$75,000	$200,000	$1,013.37	$164,813.42	$439,813.42
$100,000	$175,000	$886.70	$144,211.75	$419,211.75

The difference in interest paid is proportional to the difference in the mortgaged amounts. By increasing the down payment by $25,000, we're mortgaging 10 percent less, and the total interest paid will be about 10 percent less. A greater benefit from increasing the down payment is realized when it can be used to reduce the duration of the mortgage. In other words, increasing the down payment may lower the monthly payment enough to make a fifteen-year mortgage affordable. Then we can take advantage of the shorter duration. The table below compares the mortgage data for increased down payments.

Effects of Increasing the Down Payment Amount, 15-Year Mortgage

Down Payment	Mortgage Amount	Monthly Payment	Total Interest Paid	Total Cost of the House
$25,000	$250,000	$1,912.48	$94,246.98	$369,246.98
$50,000	$225,000	$1,721.23	$84,822.28	$359,822.28
$75,000	$200,000	$1,529.99	$75,397.59	$350,397.59
$100,000	$175,000	$1,338.74	$65,972.89	$340,972.89

To see the difference on a monthly basis, we can compare the mortgage amortization schedules. These schedules or tables list the amount of principal and interest paid and the balance of the loan on a monthly basis through the life of the mortgage. For a thirty-year mortgage, the amortization schedule will have 360 rows, since there are 360 payments. There are usually columns for the payment number, payment amount, the principle portion of the payment, the interest portion of the payment, and the balance remaining on the mortgage.

If property taxes and home owners insurance are paid by the lender (holder of the mortgage), they are usually not included on the amortization schedule. They are paid from a separate escrow (safe-keeping) account. The amount needed for the escrow account is added to our monthly payment, and the lender diverts that portion of the payment to escrow. When taxes or insurance are due, the lender pays them from that account. Since the amount needed for escrow is added to our monthly payment, we need to be sure that we understand the details of a mortgage that we're considering. The monthly payments in our examples do not include these items.

For comparison, the two tables below show the first six months of the amortization schedules for the $250,000 mortgage. The first table lists the amounts for the fifteen-year mortgage, and the second table lists the amounts for the thirty-year mortgage.

Amortization $250,000, 4.5%, 15-Year Mortgage

Payment Number	Payment Amount	Principal	Interest	Current Balance
1	$1,912.48	$974.98	$937.50	$249,025.02
2	$1,912.48	$978.64	$933.84	$248,046.38
3	$1,912.48	$982.31	$930.17	$247,064.07
4	$1,912.48	$985.99	$926.49	$246,078.08
5	$1,912.48	$989.69	$922.79	$245,088.38
6	$1,912.48	$993.40	$919.08	$244,094.98

The "current balance" column on the right is reduced faster for the fifteen-year mortgage since the principal portion of the payment is much larger. In six months, the balance on the fifteen-year mortgage has been reduced by $5,905.02. For the thirty-year mortgage (below), it has been reduced by just $1,993.89.

Amortization $250,000, 4.5%, 30-Year Mortgage

Payment Number	Payment Amount	Principal	Interest	Current Balance
1	$1,266.71	$329.21	$937.50	$249,670.79
2	$1,266.71	$330.45	$936.27	$249,340.34
3	$1,266.71	$331.69	$935.03	$249,008.65
4	$1,266.71	$332.93	$933.78	$248,675.72
5	$1,266.71	$334.18	$932.53	$248,341.54
6	$1,266.71	$335.43	$931.28	$248,006.11

People refinancing their thirty-year mortgages often opt for a fifteen-year mortgage to reduce the total amount of interest paid and to reduce the principal balance more quickly. As we've seen, the amount borrowed and the interest rate play an important role as well, so it's best to perform a thorough analysis that includes all of the variables. This could mean calculating the loan a number of times to find the best combination. Our goal is to ensure that the house is affordable over the long term and that we consider any options that could shorten the duration or lower the total interest amount paid.

In the past, mortgage lenders would scrutinize our ability to make the monthly payments based on income and debt, and they required a down payment that was at least 20 percent of the appraised value of the house (in some cases, more). These guidelines were reduced prior to the housing market crisis mentioned in the first chapter, and lenders were approving mortgages for borrowers who were making 5 percent down payments and, in some cases, no down payments at all. Although guidelines for borrowing were increased after the crisis, they have begun to ease again to promote economic growth and improve the housing market.

We should perform our own analysis and make our own financial decisions based on our financial plans and goals. Simply because a lender will loan us the money doesn't mean that it's in our best interest to borrow. Buying a home is an exciting and rewarding event in our lives, but with a long-term loan like a mortgage, we should consider much more than the monthly payment.

Credit Scores

Our credit score is a number that typically ranges between 300 and 850, and it's calculated using our credit history. A higher number is associated with a better score, and banks and lenders use credit scores to determine the credit worthiness of borrowers. There are many factors that affect our credit scores, including our borrowing history (how much we've borrowed and if it has been paid back), if we've missed payments, if we've made late payments, and our outstanding debt and credit card balances.

We should have an idea of our credit score number and review our credit report once a year to be sure that the information is accurate. Credit reports can be obtained for no charge once each year from the three major credit bureaus and annualcreditreport.com. Because of their importance, seek professional advice if you have questions or issues related to your credit score or credit history.

Chapter Summary

Eliminating debt is truly possible once we establish a realistic debt reduction plan based on our budget and discretionary income. (For convenience, the debt reduction plans are listed below.) Of course, an ounce of prevention is worth a pound of cure, and before making purchases, we need to consider whether borrowing or charging something is in line with our financial goals. There are often practical reasons for using credit, but we have to consider the cost and be sure that we understand the total amount we'll be paying with interest and carefully consider our ability to make the payments for the full duration. This is especially true for mortgages and car loans.

Debt Reduction Plans

- largest debt first
- smallest debt first
- debt with the highest interest rate first
- debt consolidation

Chapter Six

Saving

As mentioned earlier, there are three parts to our saving plan that are critical to achieving financial security: having cash on hand or a cushion for unexpected expenses, an emergency fund for a financial crisis, and a long-term saving strategy and account for our future in investments (assets such as stocks, bonds, and cash, which we'll look at in the next few chapters). This three-part approach ensures that immediate financial needs can be met, while protecting our longer-term savings. The long-term savings is protected by the emergency fund, and the emergency fund is protected by the cash on hand (cushion) account. The idea is to build walls of protection between the accounts to shield them from interruption or withdrawals.

The cushion account is held in a regular savings account at our bank for easy-access and is used for unexpected expenses, like when the refrigerator breaks or the car needs an unexpected major repair. It may contain $5,000, or you may feel comfortable with $3,000 or an amount larger than $5,000, depending on your situation.

Remember, this account is for the unexpected. If we see a new living room set and use the $5,000 in savings to buy it, then a surprise expense will need to be paid for another way. We would save separately for the living room set and always keep our cushion balance available.

Our saving plan will include regular (weekly or monthly) deposits, which is made easier if we make it automatic. Using direct deposits or automatic transfers are great ways to keep money flowing into our regular savings. In addition, many employers have payroll deduction features that allow a portion of our pay to be directly deposited into savings, or we can set up a regular bank transfer to our savings account from our checking account. The goal is to consistently make savings deposits into this cash-on-hand account and, as the balance grows, to use money from this account to supply our other accounts (covered later).

As an example, let's say that we set up a weekly, $100 direct deposit to our regular savings account. After a year, the balance is $5,200, and our cushion for unexpected expenses has been established. As time moves on and the balance continues to grow, we can move the amount above $5,000 (our cushion) from this account to our emergency fund account. Once the emergency fund has an adequate balance, we can use the excess to supply our long-term (retirement) savings account. If something unexpected happens and we need to use money from our regular savings, the account is automatically replenished through the automatic deposit.

Emergency Funds

An emergency fund (or rainy day fund) is an easily accessible (liquid) savings account with a balance equal to several months of our expenses. Several months can be three, six, or twelve depending on our comfort level, but the idea is to have an adequate amount available in case our income stops or is interrupted. Depending on our skills and the job market, it could take a few months or even a year to find another job at the same income level, and in the meantime, the bills will need to be paid.

As an example, if our total expenses each month are $6,250, then our emergency fund goal would be based on that amount (shown below). To cover expenses for three months, we would save $18,750 in the emergency fund. Then if we're more comfortable with enough to pay six months of expenses, we can raise the goal to $37,500, and so on.

Emergency Fund Amounts Using Monthly Expenses

One Month	Three Months	Six Months	One Year
$6,250	$18,750	$37,500	$75,000

This is the second layer of protection for our long-term savings and a major step toward financial independence. A money market account is typically used for the emergency fund account because they pay higher interest than regular bank savings accounts. Most have check-writing features and allow three checks to be written each month without charging a fee; some have minimum check amounts that can be written. For more information about money market accounts and features, check with your regular bank or visit the bankrate.com website.

Since the first goal in the example is to save $18,750, we establish our savings plan based on the amount that we can set aside each week from our discretionary income to save this amount. It may take some time as shown below, but don't lose heart. Every journey starts with a single step, and very often the most difficult part is getting started. The goal is to form a workable plan, begin to save (automatically if possible), and stick with it.

Time Needed to Save $18,750

Weekly deposit	$50	$100	$150	$200
Time needed	7.2 years	3.6 years	2.4 years	1.8 years

The next goal in the example is to increase the emergency fund to $37,500. Once this amount is saved, we'll have a $5,000 cushion in regular savings for unexpected expenses and an emergency fund large enough to cover expenses for six months. In addition, the savings plan is automatic through direct deposits into a regular bank savings account, and we periodically move the excess from this account to the emergency fund. Most importantly, we won't be withdrawing from either of these accounts unnecessarily.

Personal Savings

Regular bank savings account (cushion)	$5,000
Money market savings (emergency fund)	$37,500

With these two accounts established, we can begin to look at long-term savings and investing. But first, let's consider the fact that these accounts will earn interest. Although interest rates have been very low, there is still an amount being earned and added to these accounts that will help us to reach our goals. The same way that interest on credit card balances works against us, interest earned on our savings works for us. This brings us to compound interest.

Compound Interest

Simply put, compound interest is interest earned on interest that has already been earned on an account balance. Most bank savings and money market accounts provide periodic compounding of interest, and it's usually applied to the account monthly. The best way to explain the process and the benefits of compound interest is to review the growth of a deposit earning interest over time.

Let's say that our emergency fund of $37,500 has been on deposit for one year and has been earning 1 percent interest. Since 1 percent of $37,500 is $375, we might think that our end-of-year balance would be $37,875. But this equation overlooks the benefits of compounding and the fact that it is applied to the account monthly. The end-of-year balance is actually $37,876.72. Each month, interest is being earned on the balance plus the interest from the previous month.

At first glance, this might seem like a small difference, but we'll see how time and rates of return play an important role in the effects of compound interest and how this helps us reach our financial goals. Because this is so important, let's walk through what happens to the sample account for the first two months.

We'll assume that our emergency fund of $37,500 is in a money market account that pays 1 percent interest. We won't be making any additional deposits to the account. We'll just accumulate the interest earned for the example. A month later, the bank will produce a statement showing the current balance, which will no longer be $37,500 because the bank has added the interest that was earned during the month to the account. The annual (full year) interest is 1 percent of the balance in the account, which would be $375. But the interest is applied monthly, so the amount of interest that we receive for the month is essentially one-twelfth of the amount for a full year (or one month's worth of the annual interest). This results in a new balance at the end of the month of $37,531.25 as shown below.

The First Month Interest Cycle

Annual interest calculation	$37,500.00 x 1% = $375.00
Monthly interest calculation	$375.00 / 12 = $31.25

Initial balance	$37,500.00
1st month's interest	$31.25
New balance	$37,531.25

Now the interest cycle begins for the next month using the new balance of $37,531.25. Interest is earned on the new balance, which includes the interest earned during first month. The second month results are shown below.

The Second Month Interest Cycle

Annual interest calculation	$37,531.25 x 1% = $375.31
Monthly interest calculation	$375.31 / 12 = $31.28

Initial balance	$37,531.25
2nd month's interest	$31.28
New balance	$37,562.53

This monthly cycle continues, and the interest that we earn each month increases as the balance in the account continues to grow. The interest is accrued (accumulated) and added to our account balance each month, and after a full year the balance is $37,876.72.

To simplify the example, we used an interest rate of 1 percent, but the goal for a portion of our savings will be to take advantage of higher interest rates. To see the effects of higher rates, the table below lists the monthly changes to a $10,000 balance over a one-year period.

Compound Interest over 1 Year, $10,000 Balance

	Interest Rates			
Month	1%	2%	3%	4%
Jan	$10,008.33	$10,016.67	$10,025.00	$10,033.33
Feb	$10,016.67	$10,033.36	$10,050.06	$10,066.78
Mar	$10,025.02	$10,050.08	$10,075.19	$10,100.33
Apr	$10,033.38	$10,066.83	$10,100.38	$10,134.00
May	$10,041.74	$10,083.61	$10,125.63	$10,167.78
Jun	$10,050.10	$10,100.42	$10,150.94	$10,201.67
Jul	$10,058.48	$10,117.25	$10,176.32	$10,235.68
Aug	$10,066.86	$10,134.11	$10,201.76	$10,269.80
Sep	$10,075.25	$10,151.00	$10,227.26	$10,304.03
Oct	$10,083.65	$10,167.92	$10,252.83	$10,338.38
Nov	$10,092.05	$10,184.87	$10,278.46	$10,372.84
Dec	$10,100.46	$10,201.84	$10,304.16	$10,407.42

The table above shows the benefits of higher interest rates, but time is a very important factor as well. The table below shows the growth of $10,000 over longer periods of time at various interest rates. The amounts across the bottom row highlight the significant difference made by higher interest rates over longer periods.

Compound Interest over Longer Periods at Different Interest Rates

Years	1%	3%	5%	7%	9%
			Interest Rates		
0	$10,000.00	$10,000.00	$10,000.00	$10,000.00	$10,000.00
5	$10,512.49	$10,616.17	$12,833.59	$14,176.25	$15,656.81
10	$11,051.25	$13,493.53	$16,470.10	$20,096.61	$24,513.57
20	$12,213.01	$18,207.54	$27,126.42	$40,387.38	$60,091.51
30	$13,496.90	$24,568.41	$44,677.47	$81,164.99	$147,305.81

The important elements at work here are interest rate, compound interest, and time. In addition, making regular deposits to the account will have a significant impact on how quickly the balance grows. We'll look at this more closely in the next section.

Saving Larger Amounts

Earlier in the chapter, we looked at saving an emergency fund of $37,500, but for our retirement account, we might have a goal of $2,500,000 (determining this amount is covered in a later chapter). Saving an amount this large might seem impossible at first, but with regular saving, compound interest working for us, and long periods of time, we can accumulate large amounts of money.

To show how this is possible, we'll look at the accumulation of regular deposits over a longer period and then the results of the same deposits and time period with a return on investment applied.

Figure 6.1 below shows the accumulation of four different weekly deposit amounts over a thirty-five year period. There is no interest or return on investment applied in this chart. It is simply the accumulation of the weekly deposits.

Figure 6.1   Accumulation of Weekly Saving Deposits

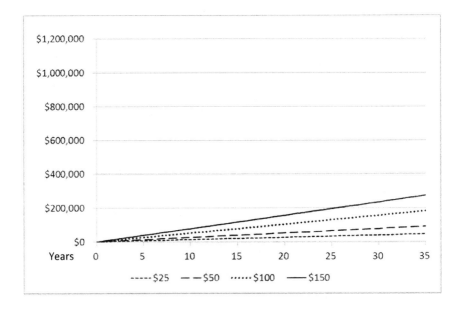

The total deposited amount over the thirty-five year period for the four weekly deposit amounts used in the figure are shown in the table below.

Total Amounts Deposited over 35 Years

Weekly Deposit	Total Amount Deposited
$25	$45,500
$50	$91,000
$100	$182,000
$150	$273,000

In contrast, figure 6.2 below shows the growth of the same weekly deposit amounts with a 7 percent average annual return on investment (or interest rate for our purposes).

Figure 6.2   Growth of Weekly Saving Deposits Earning a 7% Return on Investment

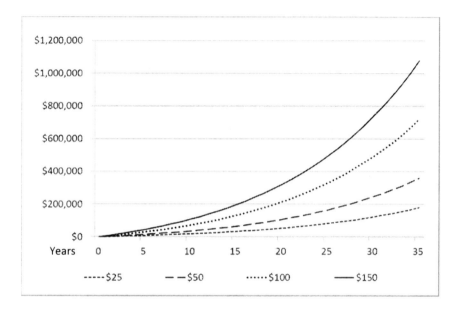

The total amounts deposited are repeated below together with the final account balances for comparison. The charts show that making regular deposits and obtaining reasonable returns over a long period of time can accumulate a significant amount of savings.

Weekly Deposit with a 7% Return on Investment over 35 Years

Weekly Deposit	Total Amount Deposited	Account Balance
$25.00	$45,500.00	$179,707.94
$50.00	$91,000.00	$359,415.88
$100.00	$182,000.00	$718,831.77
$150.00	$273,000.00	$1,078,247.65

Even though bank interest rates are extremely low, we'll see later that an average annual return on investment of 7 percent is not unrealistic. Our cushion and emergency fund accounts will most likely earn low interest rates because they are on deposit in easily accessible accounts, but our long-term savings should be earning higher returns. This will make saving a large retirement amount like $2,500,000 possible.

Let's look at some examples and determine the monthly savings amount and the time required to reach $2,500,000. We'll lower the annual return on investment to 6 percent to be more conservative and look at a few different monthly deposit amounts and a few different time periods. The table below shows that we'll need to save $1,256 each month for forty years in order to reach our $2,500,000 goal with a 6 percent average annual return. Very few people could save this amount each month.

Monthly Deposit Growth with a 6% Return on Investment

Monthly Deposit	Total Years of Saving (6% Return)				
	20	25	30	35	40
$100	$46,204	$69,299	$100,451	$142,471	$199,149
$200	$92,408	$138,599	$200,903	$284,942	$398,298
$400	$184,816	$277,198	$401,806	$569,884	$796,596
$600	$277,225	$415,796	$602,709	$854,826	$1,194,895
$1,256	$580,324	$870,401	$1,261,672	$1,789,437	$2,501,313

A more reasonable monthly saving amount might be $400, so let's recalculate the table using $400 as the deposit amount and compare the results using different rates of return over the same time periods.

There are two situations in the table below that achieve the $2,500,000 goal, but they both require an aggressive rate of return on investment and a very long time period.

Growth of $400 Monthly Savings Deposits at Different Rates of Return

Return on Investment	Total Years of Saving				
	20	25	30	35	40
8%	$235,608	$380,411	$596,144	$917,554	$1,396,404
9%	$267,155	$448,449	$732,298	$1,176,714	$1,872,529
10%	$303,748	$530,734	$904,196	$1,518,657	**$2,529,635**
11%	$346,255	$630,453	$1,121,808	$1,971,318	**$3,440,050**

If we compare the two tables, we see the relationship between the monthly deposit amount, the length of time, and the return on investment, just as we saw with interest rates previously. These are the three factors that we use to develop and monitor our long-term savings plan.

For now, let's increase the monthly saving amount and see how that affects the results. Remember, we can't increase the saving amount if we're using income to pay debt, so debt reduction is a priority. Since a $350 monthly car payment is fairly common, let's assume that our car loan was recently paid off. We could buy a new car or increase savings. Many people start a new car payment as the old one is ending or even before it's paid off, but we want to get interest working for us and not against us, so we'll keep driving the same car and add the $350 to the monthly savings in the example. This way we'll be depositing $750 each month into savings.

The table below shows the growth of the savings balance over various time periods using a monthly deposit of $750, starting with $0 invested, and receiving different annual rates of return. There are now more situations when the savings goal of $2,500,000 is reached, but again they require a long period of time and a high average rate of return.

Growth of $750 Monthly Savings Deposits at Different Rates of Return

Return on Investment	Total Years of Saving				
	20	25	30	35	40
6%	$346,531	$519,746	$753,386	$1,068,533	$1,493,618
7%	$390,695	$607,554	$914,979	$1,350,791	$1,968,611
8%	$441,765	$713,270	$1,117,769	$1,720,411	**$2,618,255**
9%	$500,915	$840,841	$1,373,057	$2,206,337	**$3,510,987**
10%	$569,527	$995,126	$1,695,368	**$2,847,482**	**$4,743,064**
11%	$649,229	$1,182,100	$2,103,390	**$3,696,222**	**$6,450,096**

We can't increase the amount of time that we have to save unless we delay retirement, and there's no guarantee that we'll receive a high rate of return year after year (we'll take a deeper look at this in the next chapter). The only controllable portions of the long-term saving equation are how soon we begin saving, the amount that we deposit, and how frequently.

Chapter Summary

It is possible to save large amounts of money when we make regular deposits and benefit from compound interest and time. To protect our savings, a cushion account in regular savings ensures that we have cash on hand to pay for unexpected expenses and establishing an emergency fund account protects against interrupted income. To make saving easier, we can make it automatic and fill the accounts one at a time either by moving the excess above our goal or by changing where the deposits are directed.

Chapter Seven

Investments

Our long-term saving plan is developed and handled very differently than the other accounts covered earlier because it has a very different purpose and involves much longer periods of time and a much larger amount of savings. In most cases, long-term savings will include an IRA and a group of investments in a diversified portfolio of stock index and bond index mutual funds. This may sound overly concise, but we'll look at each part of this statement in detail, why each part is important, and the reasons behind them. In addition, we'll review different investment terms and options and essential information about investing in general. Even if we use a professional financial advisor, these are details we should all understand.

At some point in the future, we all plan to leave the hectic work schedule and slow down, and take some form of retirement. When that time arrives, we'll be relying less on income and more on withdrawing from our savings to pay our expenses. Since retirement is a long period of time, the savings needed will be a very large amount. For instance, if my monthly expenses at retirement are $6,250, then I would need at least $75,000 each year for about thirty years.

$6,250 x 12 months = $75,000 $75,000 x 30 years = $2,250,000

Saving an amount this large is going to require a long-term saving strategy that includes regular deposits, high rates of return, and attention to anything that will increase our saving potential. Since the interest and return on investment that we earn is taxable and we're dealing with large sums of money over very long periods of time, taxes could have a significant impact on our savings. To lessen the impact, there are a couple of options worth considering, including an individual retirement account.

Individual Retirement Accounts

An individual retirement account (IRA) is a different type of savings account that we can establish for retirement savings. When we open an IRA, which can be a savings or an investment account, the taxes involved are handled differently than other accounts. We still earn interest or a return on investment, but the IRA designation gives it special tax treatment.

There are a few types of IRAs, including IRAs established by employers and self-employed individuals like simplified employee pension (SEP), and simple IRA plans. For our discussion, the most popular IRAs are traditional IRAs, Roth IRAs, and salary deferral contribution 401(k) plans which often come with a company matching contribution. Traditional IRAs and 401(k) plans allow us to deposit a limited amount of pretax income (taken from our gross pay before taxes are withheld) to an account that grows tax-deferred. Then later in life when we withdraw the money, it's taxed as though it were regular income.

With a Roth IRA, deposits are not pre-tax earnings. Income tax is paid on the money when it's earned and deposited. Then Roth IRAs grow tax deferred, and when the money is withdrawn later in life, the principal isn't taxed if certain requirements are met.

Why would I choose one over the other? If my current income and income tax bracket are high, then making deposits to a traditional IRA will lower my current income, which in turn lowers my current income tax. After retirement when my annual income (from investments or savings, a pension, or social security) is lower, I will be in a lower income tax bracket. Then I can make withdrawals from the IRA and pay a lower income tax rate on the withdrawals. If I believe that my income will be the same or higher in retirement, I might want to use a Roth IRA and pay the income tax now and not later in life when I withdraw.

Either type can be a tax-efficient way to save for the future, but due to regular changes in tax laws, consult the latest information and an accountant, or financial advisor when opening an IRA account. Both IRAs have penalties for early (unqualified) withdrawals, and there are limits to the amount we can deposit each year. There are pros and cons with each type of IRA, so investigate which is best for you.

Since most IRAs are invested in some type of security (stocks, bonds, mutual funds, etc.), an understanding of each type of investment is important. Also, don't assume that your employer has invested your IRA or 401(k) in your best interest. If your retirement savings is handled through your employer, spend some time understanding the investment options in the plan to be sure your investments are in line with your goals. Investment options will be covered in the next few sections.

Stocks

Explaining company stocks could fill a book of its own, but we'll cover the basics that anyone with investments should know. Stocks are essentially pieces of ownership in a company. They're often called shares or equities, and companies sell stock to obtain cash that they don't have to repay. When a company sells or issues a bond, they are committing to pay interest on the bond and repay the original bond amount at some point in the future. When companies borrow money in the form of loans, again they pay interest on the loan and must repay the amount borrowed. When we buy shares of stock in a company, we're not lending the company our money. The company is not obligated to buy the stock back from us. We're purchasing part ownership in the company, and we become shareholders.

There is no limit to the number of shares that a company can sell, but usually when they sell additional shares, they try to have the least amount of impact on their current stock price. Companies also buy back their stock from time to time to decrease the number of shares outstanding, and this tends to increase the price of the shares on the market in the short term.

There are two main types of stock: preferred stock and common stock. Owning *preferred* company stock often comes with certain privileges like a periodic dividend (distributions of company earnings, which we'll cover later), and in the case of bankruptcy or liquidation, repayment ahead of common stock owners (after creditors). Preferred shareholders usually do not have voting rights (common stockholders vote for company board members and other issues in annual meetings) and don't tend to appreciate in price.

Common stock owners, also called shareholders, expect to share in the profits of the company and earn a return on their investment either through dividends (covered next) or by realizing gains (capital gains) through an increase in the price of the shares they own. Of course, it doesn't always work out this way. A company is not obligated to pay dividends, and a stock's price may rise or fall.

For the purposes of this book, "stock" will always refer to common stock: the stocks that are bought and sold (traded) on the stock exchanges and make up most mutual fund investments.

Dividends

Dividends are payments made by companies to shareholders from the profits that the company earns. Companies often reinvest their profits by buying buildings, equipment, or services, but some pay a dividend to their shareholders (shareholders are *sharing* in the profits of the company). Companies that pay dividends tend to be large, stable companies like Johnson & Johnson or General Electric, and because of their large size, their growth tends to be small in comparison to the growth of smaller companies. This usually translates into smaller increases in the price of the shares of their stock, so investors in these companies are often more interested in the dividend they will receive by owning the stock.

There is no guarantee that a dividend will be paid to shareholders. The decision to pay a dividend and the size of the dividend are made by the company's board of directors. If a company that typically pays a dividend announces that it's going to stop or lower its dividend amount, it might be an indicator of a financial or business issue. Dividend stock investors look for companies that consistently pay dividends without interruption, and when dividends are paid, they can be paid directly to us or reinvested in more stock in the company.

There are many companies that do not pay dividends to common stockholders. They reinvest their profits back into the company to grow their business (increase sales and profits). When a business is growing, the price of their stock (share price) tends to rise. Investors buy stock in these companies to earn the profit from buying them at a certain price and selling them at a higher price.

Although stocks typically provide much higher returns than other investments either through dividends, an increase in the share price, or both, there is also a risk that the price will decrease. Very often increases and decreases in stock prices persist over a period. When stock prices in general rise faster than their historical average over an extended period of time, the market is said to be a bull market. When prices are falling faster than their historical average for an extended period, the market is said to be a bear market. This can happen for variety of reasons as we'll see in the next section.

Share Price

Since a share of stock is part ownership in a company, we might think that the price per share is based on what the company is worth. For instance, if company ABC is worth $1 million, and there are one million shares of stock outstanding, then we might think that each share would be worth $1.00. But it's not this simple. In fact, the *market* value of a company (or market capitalization) is based on the share price and not the other way around.

Market capitalization = Stock price x Number of shares outstanding

Since stock prices fluctuate continuously, if the price of ABC's stock rises to $2.00 per share, and there are one million shares outstanding, then the market capitalization is $2 million. The company's worth hasn't changed from $1 million; only the company's market capitalization has changed as a result of the new stock price.

Basically, companies can be divided into three categories by market capitalization: large, medium, and small. They're referred to as large-cap, mid-cap, and small-cap and are typically divided as shown below.

Standard Market Capitalization Categories

Large-cap	Higher than $10 billion
Mid-cap	$2 billion to $10 billion
Small-cap	Less than $2 billion

Essentially, there is no direct connection between the share price for a company's stock and the company's worth. The company's *actual* worth is based on many things that the company owns including buildings, trucks, equipment, and patents on technology. In addition, a company has existing customers, generates income through sales, and has a forecast for future sales and profits. To determine a company's true worth, all of these factors would need to be considered as well as the potential for growth in terms of sales and profits. This can be extremely difficult to determine.

Since a company's stock price also reflects the future growth (increase in sales and profits) of the company, like any forecast, this can be very subjective and can add an emotional dimension to the stock price. If a lot of people *think* that a company will do very well in the future, and they start buying large amounts of the stock, the price will tend to rise. The law of supply and demand will have an effect. If there is a demand for a particular stock and not enough people are willing to sell their shares, then the price will rise until someone is willing to sell their shares and the demand is satisfied. If you happen to own the stock while this is happening, then your shares become more valuable. If the price rises higher than the price that you paid, you can sell at the higher price and make a profit.

The opposite could also happen. If a lot of people want to sell the shares that they own in a particular company and there aren't enough buyers, then the price will fall until people are willing to buy the stock. If you happen to own shares in the company while this is happening, then the price of your shares will be affected as well. If you don't sell your shares, then only the *value* of your shares has changed. You could keep the shares, hoping that the price will rise again, but you haven't lost any money unless you sell at the lower price.

At any point in time, the value of our investment account is the number of shares that we own multiplied by the current stock price, and the price of a share of stock is simply the price that someone else is willing to pay for it at the time … its current selling price. These are the prices that we see in newspapers and stock market quotes.

Consider if we owned stock in two different companies, and one company's stock is rising in price and the other is falling. To some degree, the increase and decrease would be offset. But there's also a risk that they could both fall in price at the same time. If we increase our investment to include stock in three different companies, the chance that all three would fall in price is somewhat less. As we increase the number of companies in our investment, we continue to reduce the risk that all or even most of the stock will fall in price at the same time. This is a form of diversification.

Investing in many stocks and many companies is simplified by buying shares in a mutual fund. By investing in a mutual fund, we can essentially own an investment in five hundred companies (or more) without buying each stock. This diversifies (spreads) our investment across stocks in many companies. A few may rise in value and a few may lose value, but the chance that all, or even most, of the companies in the fund will lose value over a long period is not consistent with historical market returns.

When we hear that the stock market returns an average of 10–12 percent over long periods of time, this refers to historical market returns for a very large portion of the market. In the chapter on mutual funds, we'll look at how to take advantage of this trend by investing in very large segments. For further reading on the subject, *A Random Walk Down Wall Street* by Burton G. Malkiel provides historical information about the stock market and market returns. It's an insightful journey through market trends and periods of highs, lows, and abnormalities.

Ticker Symbols

Since there are hundreds of thousands of companies, we use unique identifiers called ticker symbols (usually a group of letters) to refer to their stock without confusion. These are used in stock listings in publications as a sort of abbreviation for a company's stock. The ticker symbol for Johnson & Johnson, mentioned previously, is JNJ. Ticker symbols can be used to quickly locate information about a company's stock on the Internet or in newspapers and magazines.

Bonds

Bonds are long-term debt instruments (essentially loans) used by businesses and governments to raise large sums of money. Most people are familiar with US Government Savings Bonds, but there are many other kinds including those sold by companies and municipalities. As an example, a large company may want to borrow $1 billion, but there aren't many places to borrow an amount that large. The company could sell (or issue) $1 billion worth of bonds, and by buying them, we're loaning the company our money. This loan we're making comes with a promised interest payment or interest rate (often called the coupon rate) and a promise that we'll be repaid our initial investment.

For example, with a $10,000, 5 percent, eight-year company bond, the company promises to pay us $500 each year in interest plus return the $10,000 in principal (that we paid to buy the bond) in eight years (at maturity). The 5 percent interest rate is fixed and will not go up or down. This is why bonds are called fixed-income investments. Unless the company defaults on the bond due to a financial crisis, we will receive $500 each year for eight years, and then we will be repaid our $10,000 initial investment.

There are many kinds of bonds—short-term, long-term, treasury bonds, municipal bonds, junk bonds (bonds with a high risk of default, meaning we might lose our money)—and many levels of bond ratings (sort of a credit score for bond issuers). Junk bonds, for instance, have a low credit rating and a higher risk associated with owning them. This is why they have the potential for a higher return. I say potential because the company could default, and we could lose our investment.

Government savings bonds would have a high credit rating and a very low risk rating, but the return on investment (or interest rate) is also low. To assess the risks associated with bonds, bond ratings are performed and published by private companies (Moody's, Standard & Poor's, and others). The ratings are based on the bond issuer's estimated ability to repay principal and interest on their debt, including bonds. The companies that assess bonds publish the bond ratings that we see in newspapers and financial periodicals using rating indicators. Government bonds would typically be rated AAA (very high), and junk bonds would typically have a D rating (very low).

Although there are many types of bonds, for our purposes, bonds will always refer to low–risk (high grade) corporate and government bonds, and will always refer to short-, intermediate-, or long-term bonds. The term refers to the period until maturity as shown in the table below.

Bond Maturity Groups

Term	Short	Intermediate	Long
Maturity	1–3 years	4–6 years	7–10 years

Many investors choose low-risk, highly rated, intermediate-term bonds for the bond portion of their investments. Highly rated bonds are chosen because there is more assurance they'll receive the interest payments and be repaid the principal (initial cost) at maturity. They choose intermediate-term because these bonds are less subject to the effects of inflation and interest rates because it's maturing in about five years.

Here are a few examples to show why an intermediate term is often preferred by investors. If we own a long-term bond paying 2 percent interest and inflation rises to 2.5 percent, then our investment isn't keeping up with inflation (shown below). We would be earning less in interest than inflation is taking away, and we're in a long-term commitment.

Bond Interest and Inflation

Bond interest rate	2.0%
Inflation rate	2.5%
Inflation adjusted return on investment	– 0.5%

If interest rates are rising, the bond is locked into the lower interest rate until it matures. The bond could be sold, but at a lower price because it isn't paying the same interest as other bonds on the market.

With a short-term bond, if interest rates are falling we'll be reinvesting the money in a new bond at a lower interest rate when the bond matures. To reduce the risk of changes in interest rates effecting bond investments, and to ensure that some cash is available, some investors establish a plan called bond laddering.

Laddering

Laddering is a method used to ensure that some bonds are maturing on a regular basis. The maturities or durations for the bonds are staggered using different terms at first; as they mature, they're replaced with similar maturities.

For example, let's say that we purchase five different bonds. One bond matures in one year, another matures in two years, another in three, another in four, and another in five years. Each year when a bond matures, we reinvest in a new five-year bond. Eventually, we have a portfolio of five-year bonds, with a bond maturing every year. If we need our money to pay expenses or interest rates have changed for the worse, we can choose the option that fits our financial plan.

Laddering still ties up our money at the bond's interest rate until it matures, but only a portion of our total investment is tied up in each bond, and we have a bond maturing every year.

Bond Returns

The return on investment for bonds is usually higher than a bank savings account, and many people have their long-term investments exclusively in bonds. If we invest solely in bonds, then our returns will be directly impacted by changes in interest rates and inflation. This could be good or bad, depending on the economy.

To compare the long-term returns for the three different bond maturity levels, figure 7.1 shows the hypothetical growth of $10,000 invested in the Vanguard short-term, intermediate-term, and long-term bond market index funds over a ten year period. Economic changes, including inflation and interest rates, affect bond prices and bond returns. Although inflation remained relatively constant over the period, changes in interest rates affected returns in the later years. Prior to that, there was only a small difference in the growth of the investments. When we review the past performance of an investment, we should consider the economic conditions of the time period.

Figure 7.1   Bond Market Index Fund Performance

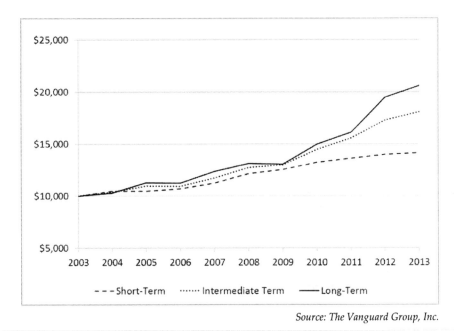

Source: The Vanguard Group, Inc.

Stocks and Bonds

The return on investment history of stocks and bonds shows that they are loosely correlated, meaning their prices or performances tend to move in different directions in the market. Figure 7.2 below shows the ten-year hypothetical growth of $10,000 invested in the Vanguard Total Bond Market Index Fund and the Vanguard 500 Index Fund, which contains five hundred large company stocks. Notice that the total bond market investment experienced steady growth even when the stock investment declined sharply during the housing market crisis. The stock fund outperformed the bond fund, but only during certain periods.

Figure 7.2 Vanguard Total Bond Market and Total Stock Market Index Funds

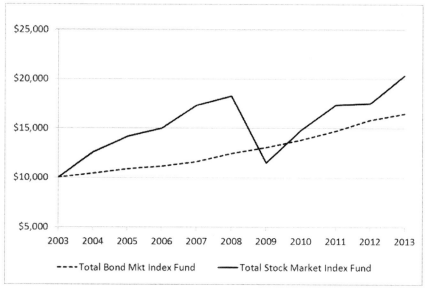

Source: *The Vanguard Group, Inc.*

Trying to determine ahead of time exactly when to be invested in stocks or bonds would be impossible. We would end up switching investments in the hope that we have our money invested in the right place at the right time. Since inflation, changes in the economy, and many other factors affect the prices and returns of stocks and bonds in different ways, putting them together gives us a mix that produces average returns using both assets.

Chapter Summary

With a basic understanding of investments, we're better equipped to develop our long-term savings plan. Achieving financial goals that include large amounts of money will require a greater return on investment than the interest paid by our bank savings account, and we can take advantage of the long-term averages for stock and bond market returns. The more that we know about investments and how they perform, the more comfortable we are with conservative investing and we're less likely to over-react during temporary market fluctuations. In addition, we'll see in the next chapter on mutual funds, how we can diversify our investments to further reduce risk to our savings.

Chapter Eight

Mutual Funds

Mutual funds are a type of investment made up of a pool of money from many investors. The mutual fund uses the large pool of money to purchase a wide range of stocks and bonds that no single investor could own individually. We invest in the mutual fund and gain investment access to the portfolio of investments within the fund. This way, with a limited amount of money to deposit, we can invest in many securities (hundreds or thousands of stocks or bonds). Our investment is diversified across many securities, even though we're invested in a single fund.

Each mutual fund has a prospectus that describes the portfolio structure (types of investments the fund buys), lists the individual investments within the fund, and explains the investment objectives of the fund. In addition, each fund is operated by a fund manager who is responsible for managing the fund and meeting the objectives. Mutual fund company websites provide all of the information about their funds in a variety of formats and have extensive search functions to make it easier to locate a specific fund.

Since our investment goal is broad diversification and average market volatility and returns, we can select funds that invest in large segments of the market like the total stock market or total bond market and take advantage of low-cost index funds (covered later).

Ticker Symbols (Again)

As mentioned earlier, ticker symbols are unique identifiers for stocks, but they're also used to identify mutual funds. There are thousands of mutual funds and many mutual fund companies. Since many companies have similar funds, the fund names are often similar. The ticker symbol makes it easier to locate information about a particular fund, as well as past performance data from financial websites or in newspapers and periodicals. Below are the fund names and ticker symbols for a variety of Vanguard mutual funds for reference.

Example: Ticker Symbols—Vanguard Mutual Funds

Ticker Symbol	Fund Name
VTSMX	Total (US) Stock Market Index Fund
VFINX	500 Index Fund
VLACX	Large-Cap Index Fund
VIMSX	Mid-Cap Index Fund
NAESX	Small-Cap Index Fund
VGTSX	Total International Stock Index Fund
VFWIX	FTSE All-World ex-US Index
VDMIX	Developed Markets Index
VEIEX	Emerging Markets Stock Index
VEURX	European Stock Index
VBMFX	Total Bond Market Index
VBISX	Short-Term Bond Index
VBIIX	Intermediate-Term Bond Index
VBLTX	Long-Term Bond Index
VFIIX	GNMA Fund

Source: The Vanguard Group, Inc.

Mutual Fund Costs

A good indicator of the overall costs that we pay (indirectly) to invest in a mutual fund is the fund's expense ratio. The expense ratio is the fund's total operating expenses as a percentage of fund assets, and it relates directly to our return on investment because the costs are taken from the fund's assets. A lower expense ratio is best, and a good range would be 0.11–0.50 percent. Costs to invest in mutual funds that are not included in the expense ratio are loads and transaction fees, which we'll discuss below.

Mutual fund loads are fees that are charged by some funds when we initially invest (front-end load) or when we withdraw completely from the fund (back-end load). As an example, if we deposit $4,000 in a front-end load fund charging $200, our initial balance would be $3,800 because the $200 load is removed from our deposit (at the front end). If there's a back-end load, then it will be removed from our withdrawal when we exit the fund. Sometimes loads are a percentage of our investment amount, and some loads are waived if the investment amount we're depositing is large. If a fund has a load, the information can be found on the fund's website or at Morningstar.com.

Many funds have additional costs like 12b-1 fees (distribution or marketing fees), commissions, management fees, or account service fees. These costs of operating, managing, and marketing a fund reduce our return on investment and don't provide any benefit to the investors.

In the sections ahead where we'll look at return on investment, keep these costs and fees in mind. If we add up all of the fees associated with some funds, the totals range from 1–2.5 percent and could severely reduce our returns. As an example, if we invest for one year in a large-cap stock fund that has management fees of 1.5 percent, and the large-cap market returns 7.2 percent, then in order to produce a return equal to the market, the fund manager will have to produce a return that is 8.7 percent or higher in order to cover the management and transaction fees. If not, then our return from the fund will be less than the average market return. We'll discuss this further in the section on index mutual funds.

When researching funds and fund companies, be sure to uncover all of the charges and fees before investing. Fund companies and brokers are in business to make money, so we need to do our homework. Many companies claim to have low fees, so be sure to read the fine print. As our portfolio balance grows, management fees and costs can become significant amounts of money.

To highlight the impact of fund costs, the table below shows various expense ratios and the cost incurred in one year for a $350,000 portfolio.

Example Fees for a $350,000 Portfolio

Expense Ratio	Cost to the Investor
0.18%	$630
0.25%	$875
0.60%	$2,100
0.80%	$2,800
1.20%	$4,200
1.50%	$5,250
1.80%	$6,300
2.10%	$7,350
2.50%	$8,750

Any area where we can reduce the costs of investing is worth consideration, and since fund companies provide fee– and tax–related information, it's very easy to compare them. One mutual fund company that's popular among fee-conscious investors is The Vanguard Group, which is owned by the investors. The company does not make a profit from operating their funds, and the costs associated with their mutual funds are among the lowest in the industry.

As an example, the expense ratio for the Vanguard Total Stock Market Index Fund is currently 0.17 percent and has no sales loads, no 12b-1 distribution or marketing fees, and no account service fees with electronic statements. Because of lower fees, the influx of investments into Vanguard funds has been significant ($130.4 billion in 2012).

Index Mutual Funds

An index (or market index) is a grouping or list of financial securities (stocks, bonds, etc.) created to measure the performance of a specific segment of the market. These points of reference or benchmarks show us how the market or certain segments of the market are performing. For example, if we wanted to know the price performance for all of the large US company stocks, we might put together a list or grouping of five hundred large companies. We would then measure the performance of each company's stock over some period of time and combine the information into a measure of large company stock performance.

To save us the trouble, financial rating agencies create various groupings like this and track the performance of the stocks or bonds within the group. These groupings are called indexes, and their performance is published, so we have a single point of reference to judge the day-to-day, week-to-week, or year-to-year performance of segments of the market. If we want to know how technology, small, large, or foreign stocks are performing, there are indexes that track those segments (and many more).

The same is true of bonds. There are short-, intermediate-, and long-term bond indexes, and even an index for the total bond market. If we see that the returns for a particular index are consistently good, then we might want to invest in the assets that comprise the index. To do this, we can invest in an index mutual fund designed for that particular index.

Active and Passive Management

There are tens of thousands of mutual funds, but essentially two kinds: those that are actively managed and those that are passively managed (indexed). *Actively* managed fund managers use research, market forecasts, and judgment to select stocks or bonds (securities) to buy and sell in an attempt to maximize returns. Buying and selling the assets of a fund is called turnover, and there are costs (transaction fees) associated with each transaction. A fund's turnover rate can tell us how much buying and selling is going on and whether the transaction costs for the fund might be high (which reduces our returns).

The turnover rate for many actively managed funds is over 100 percent, meaning that all of the fund's assets are sold and replaced in a year. The management fees and transaction costs affect the returns, and these funds seldom perform better than average market returns. People invest in them because they have produced higher returns on occasion, and many investors like having someone actively managing the funds in their investments.

Passively managed funds attempt to match or track a market index and are typically called index mutual funds. Their portfolios are comprised of the stocks or bonds that make up the index in the same proportions (weighting) as the index. Since there is very little turnover in an index and the fund doesn't require active management, index funds have much lower expenses and tend to produce returns similar to the index they track. Most mutual fund companies have index funds that track the more popular indexes (a few are shown below).

Popular Indexes

- The S&P 500 Index—comprised of the most widely held large company stocks (Standard & Poor's 500).

- The Dow Jones Industrial average (DOW)—represents about a quarter of the over-all US stock market capitalization (the largest companies). Yet, out of the more than three thousand company stocks traded on Wall Street, the Dow Jones Industrial Average is made up of only thirty very large industrial company stocks.

- NASDAQ Composite Index—comprised of over three thousand US and non-US stocks and is regarded as the indicator of the performance of technology and growth companies. Only companies exclusively listed on the NASDAQ Stock Exchange are included in the composite.

- Russell 1000 Index—index of about one thousand of the largest US companies.

- Russell 2000 Index—index of about two thousand small US companies.

- Russell 3000 Index—essentially the Russell 1000 and 2000 combined.

- Wilshire 5000 Total Stock Market Index—6,700 US companies; attempts to track the entire US market

- MSCI EAFE Index—(MSCI) Morgan Stanley Composite Index (EAFE) Europe, Australasia (Australia and Asia), and the Far East.

- MSCI ACWI Index—(ACWI) All World Country Index, nine thousand stocks of large, mid-sized, and small companies in forty-five developed and emerging foreign countries.

If we wanted to invest in a very large portion of the market, we might invest in a fund that tracks the Russell 3000 or Wilshire 5000. The fund would be composed of those stocks making up the index in proportion to their market capitalization (the price of each stock multiplied by the number of common stock shares outstanding). For a small amount of money, we could invest in the fund and be invested in three thousand or five thousand stocks (sort of). This would diversify our investment across many different company stocks. Again, we wouldn't own the stock in the companies; we would own shares in the mutual fund that owns the stock in the companies.

ETFs and Other Investment Variations

From time to time, investment variations are created in the financial industry—for example, exchange traded funds or ETFs. As the name implies, ETF shares are traded similar to stocks on the stock exchanges even though they're funds. Their prices and performance are affected as shares are bought and sold in the market, and they're typically passive like index mutual funds, although a couple of actively managed ETFs have been created. The fees associated with them tend to be very low, and they must be bought and sold through a broker, which incurs a broker's fee for the transaction.

There are many varieties of ETFs and other investment vehicles to offer investors more options, including derivatives, hedge funds, futures, exchange-traded contracts, and a host of other variations. Different investment types tend to rise and fall in popularity among investors from time to time, and we often hear about a great new investment opportunity. The important thing to remember is that we should never commit any of our money unless we completely understand an investment. We need to do our own homework.

Dollar-Cost Averaging

Making regular deposits of the same amount into an investment account is typically referred to as dollar-cost averaging. With this approach, the amount is deposited to the account weekly or monthly without considering the price of the investment in the buying decision. Investing through dollar-cost averaging ensures that we're saving regularly, and it actually uses price changes in the investment to our advantage. Since we're always depositing the same amount, when the price of the asset is low, we're buying more, and when the price is higher, we're buying less.

In a perfect scenario, we would only buy when prices are low, but we can never know the price that an investment will be in the future, only what it has been. Oddly, when prices are falling, a lot of investors get nervous and sell, and when prices start going up, they try to take advantage of the upward trend and buy. What often happens is that they sell their investment at a loss when the price is falling and then buy at a higher price when it's rising. They're also paying transaction fees for buying and selling, and the result is usually lower returns.

Figure 8.1 shows the hypothetical growth of $10,000 invested in the Vanguard 500 Index Fund for the year 2012. As the data shows, stock prices can vary significantly over short periods, and we need to stay focused on our long-term strategy. An investor who reacted to the decline in April by selling their investments would have missed the gains through the rest of the year.

Figure 8.1   Vanguard 500 Index Fund 2012

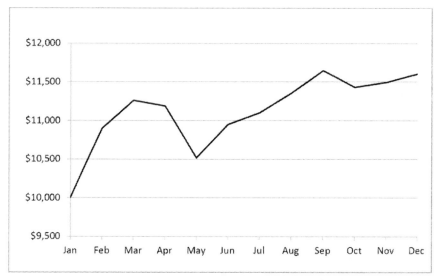

Source: The Vanguard Group, Inc.

Dollar-cost averaging takes the guesswork out of when to buy investments, because we're always buying—just in different quantities. The table below shows the changes in the number of shares purchased as a result of dollar-cost averaging using $1000 deposits in an account invested in a total US stock market index fund.

Dollar-cost Averaging

Share Price	Deposit	Shares Purchased
$23.50	$1000.00	42.6
$21.19	$1000.00	47.2
$18.60	$1000.00	53.8

If we have our cushion savings account and emergency fund in place and fully funded, we can direct regular deposits to our long-term savings (investments). Dollar-cost averaging shows that investing using this method doesn't hurt us. In fact, it helps.

Mutual Fund Returns

If we're invested in index mutual funds, our return on investment should closely match the index that the fund is tracking, minus any management fees. The fund's long-term average return information is available at fund websites and at Morningstar.com (just keep in mind that past performance is no guarantee of the future). But there is some risk, which we'll discuss further in the next chapter. A few long-term average returns are shown in the table below for reference.

Fund	10-Year Average Annual Performance
Total Stock Market Index Fund	9.31%
500 Index Fund	8.42%
Total International Stock Index Fund	10.62%
Total Bond Market Index Fund	4.93%

Source: The Vanguard Group, Inc.

Chapter Summary

Mutual funds provide a way for us to invest in widely diversified segments of the stock and bond markets. We don't own the actual stocks or bonds in the mutual fund; we own shares in the fund, which owns the company stocks or bonds. When selecting funds, we should look for low costs: a low expense ratio; no loads; low transaction fees (low turnover ratio); and no 12b-1 fees (distribution or marketing fees), commissions, management fees, or account service fees. These costs reduce our return on investment and don't provide any benefits.

Actively managed fund managers attempt to maximize returns by using market research, analysis, forecasts, and judgment to select stocks or bonds to buy and sell. These funds usually have high turnover ratios and expenses. Passively managed (index) funds buy and hold the stocks or bonds in the index they are tracking. They typically have very little turnover and low expenses, and they tend to produce returns similar to the index they track.

From time to time, the financial industry creates new investment variations to offer investors additional options. The important thing to remember is that we should never invest our money in anything that we don't completely understand.

Making regular deposits of the same amount into an investment account is called dollar-cost averaging, since the same amount is invested each period without regard to the cost of the asset. More shares of the investment are purchased when the price is low, and less shares are purchased when the price is higher. This actually works in our favor.

Chapter Nine

Risk and Return

As mentioned before, the performances of various segments of the market tend to move in different directions. They're said to have a low correlation. On the other hand, segments of the market that tend to move in the same direction are said to have a high correlation. Investing in stocks in only one portion of the market like small-cap, or in similar types of company stocks like utility companies, puts our investment at the mercy of that particular portion of the market (all of our eggs are in one basket). The same is true of mutual funds. Two funds made up of similar assets will tend to move in the same direction (they are highly correlated). It is true that if we invest in only one area of the market and that particular area performs very well, we could reap high profits, but the opposite could happen just as well. To offset this possibility, we invest in assets that have typically shown a low correlation in reaction to market and economic changes.

In addition to different types of domestic stocks, foreign stocks and domestic stocks tend to have a low correlation and so do stocks and bonds. When the US stock market is rising, foreign markets tend to be stagnant or are falling, and vice versa. When the stock market is performing well, the bond market tends to stagnate or lose value. There are always exceptions to the rule and predicting the future of the market is impossible, but this is generally how market segments have performed historically.

As an example, using the monthly price data from 2012 for the Vanguard Total Stock Market Index and Total Bond Market Index Funds, the hypothetical growth of $10,000 invested in each is plotted in figure 9.1. In the early months when stock performance was poor, bonds maintained positive growth, but the situation reversed in the later months.

Figure 9.1   Total Stock Market Index and Total Bond Market Index Funds

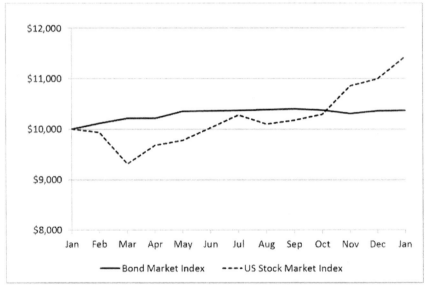

Source: Vanguard Group, Inc.

Many factors affect market performance, including domestic and foreign economies; unemployment, inflation, and other issues that impact the business climate; company profits; and investor reactions to the news media. All of these will have an effect on stock prices, bond prices, bond interest, the price of precious metals (gold, silver, etc.), and the movement and performance of the markets. As an investor, we can either guess at what to buy and sell and when to buy and sell (and pay the commissions to buy and sell), or we can diversify our investments so we're not exposed too much in any one area or segment and ride out the short-term gyrations and volatility of the market.

Diversifying across markets tends to dampen the volatility of our portfolio as the market goes through its temporary ups and downs. This provides a certain amount of stability for the portfolio as a whole, even if some of the assets within the portfolio are fluctuating in price.

Figure 9.1 above also shows the volatility of the two assets. Volatility is essentially the spread between the high and low prices, or upward and downward swings. An investment with wide price swings is considered to be highly volatile and more risky. As shown in the figure, the bond index fund had the least amount of volatility and lower risk (and the least amount of increase, or lowest performance). The stock index fund displayed more volatility and greater performance. Many investors prefer lower volatility levels, and they're willing to accept the potential for lower return on investment. The least volatile investment would be a bank savings account.

Within the US stock market, certain stocks tend to be more volatile than others. One example would be small-cap (small capitalization) stocks. Historically, smaller company stocks tend to rise higher and fall lower than the market as a whole. Small companies also tend to grow more quickly than larger companies, and when economic factors are favorable, their stocks tend to perform very well. But small companies are also more vulnerable to economic declines, whereas large companies tend to be more stable in poor economic periods due to their size and long-established products and customers. Large company stock prices also tend to rise more gradually when the market is rising.

Foreign stocks tend to be more volatile than domestic stocks. And within the category of foreign stocks, emerging-country (emerging-market) stocks tend to be more volatile than developed-country (developed-market) stocks. Of course, there are times when stock prices move abnormally, but on average they tend to perform this way.

When an investment is more volatile than another, we expect a greater return on our investment because we're assuming more risk with our money, and it often works out this way. There is a risk-return relationship in investing where more volatile or risky investments tend to provide a greater return.

Risk and Return

Most of the investments that we're covering are not insured by the FDIC (Federal Deposit Insurance Corporation), which guarantees bank deposits, or the NCUA (National Credit Union Administration), which insures deposits in credit unions. There is no risk that we could lose the money that we have on deposit at our bank (up to certain limits) or credit union, but with investments, it's quite different. The trade-off that we make for the safety of insured accounts is the lower interest rate that they pay. On the other hand, when we invest in mutual funds, stocks, and most bonds, our investment is not insured or guaranteed. There is a risk that we could lose some or all of our investment, and therefore we expect (and typically receive) a greater return on our investment.

The risk-return relationship is at work in all financial transactions. When there is a greater chance that we could lose our money, we expect the chance for a greater return than we might expect from a less risky investment. When there's a reasonable chance that we could lose all of our investment (such as investments in junk bonds), we want to be compensated with the opportunity to receive a much higher return. To reduce the amount of risk to our investments, we use what we know about the performance of different stocks and bonds and create a mixed portfolio that diversifies some of the risk away from the individual investments.

We might think that a portfolio made up entirely of bonds would have the lowest risk, but being solely invested in bonds is actually more risky than a mix of stocks and bonds. This is because interest rates and inflation have an effect on bonds that adds some risk when they're held by themselves. We remove some of this risk to our portfolio (not to the bonds), by including an investment in some stocks.

Similarly, a portfolio invested solely in stocks has the potential for the highest return, but it also has the most volatility and risk. Mixing investments in our portfolio that move in different directions lessens the risk to the portfolio (we won't have all of our eggs in one basket). Somewhere between a bond-only portfolio and a stock-only portfolio is our proper asset mix. It depends on how much risk we're willing to take to obtain our expected return on investment.

Consider Figure 9.1 again and imagine if half of your invested money was in each of the funds. When stock prices were falling, the bond portion of your investment would still be performing. When the stock portion rebounded late in the year, you would probably be glad you had kept that investment. We want our portfolio to provide the greatest return at what we feel is our comfort level for risk and volatility. If we're constantly worried about how the stock market is acting and we're losing sleep over it, then investing in further diversified or a less volatile mix of assets is probably a good idea.

Diversification

Diversification to reduce volatility can go beyond just mixing stocks and bonds. We can also diversify within the stock portion of our investments. There are small, medium, and large company stocks in both the US and in foreign countries, and the stock markets can be (and are) sliced a thousand ways. There are technology stocks, utility stocks, energy stocks, and many others, and there are mutual funds for practically any segment of the market. We can get lost in all the choices, but our goal is broad exposure to the markets without our portfolio being weighted too heavily toward any one market segment. We develop a long-term investment strategy with an appropriate mix of assets that provides our desired return at a comfortable risk level. We'll look at diversified portfolio composition in the next chapter.

Risk and Speculating

We've confined our discussion to long-term investing, which takes a large and long view of the market. It's methodical and long-term trend oriented, and that's why mutual funds have been our focus. They're diversified due to their size and scope, and they provide reasonable returns over long periods of time. Speculating, on the other hand, is buying an item for the short term, hoping it will rise in price quickly, and then selling it at a profit.

Speculating attempts to take advantage of a major company event that might occur, like a new technology or drug that a company invented that the FDA (Food and Drug Administration) is expected to approve for sale in the near future. These events could have a positive effect on the company's stock price, and speculators will buy the stock, hoping that the price will rise. If it does, they can sell and earn a profit. In some cases, stocks are bought by speculators and only owned for weeks, days, or even hours before they're sold. Since there is often a transaction fee when we buy and sell stock, the profit made by speculating must be high enough to cover the transaction costs.

In the 1990s, speculating took on a whole new meaning as Internet-based stock trading companies allowed people to set up their own accounts and to buy and sell (trade) shares over the Internet. Many people started trading stocks regularly themselves, and people were buying stocks in the morning and selling them in the afternoon at a profit. Stock prices were increasing rapidly, especially technology company stocks, and as more and more people heard about it, many more got involved.

The media quickly got in the game, and the stock market and the latest stock prices became the hottest news items. It seemed that everyone was investing and trading stocks almost daily. This trend quickly became known as day-trading, and some people even quit their jobs so that they could stay at home and buy and sell stocks all day online, hoping to make their fortune.

Since most of this fast-paced buying and selling activity was in technology company stocks trading on the NASDAQ exchange, the event came to be known as the "tech-stock bubble" or "dot-com bubble." Any company with "tech" in its name was a hot stock, even if the company had nothing to do with technology or had never even sold a product. New companies were being created daily on the Internet, and people were buying their stock as soon as it was available. Older companies were changing their names to include something technical so that they could benefit from what was happening. Stock prices soared higher and higher as shown in the center of figure 9.2 below.

Figure 9.2   Tech-Stock Bubble of the Late 1990s—Composite Index

Data Source: Wikipedia

When the dot-com bubble popped and stock prices collapsed, it ended badly for a lot of people and a lot of companies. Many people panicked as prices fell, and they sold their stocks at huge losses. Others saw the companies they invested in go bankrupt and the stock they owned become worthless. For a very few people who bought and sold at the right time, the rewards were very high, but as we can see from the chart, so were the risks.

If we want to have the fun and excitement of some speculating, we should never use more than 10 percent of our portfolio, separate the funds from our other accounts, never mix speculating with long-term investments, and never confuse the two strategies.

Chapter Summary

Various segments of the stock and bond markets tend to move in different directions in reaction to economic changes. They're said to have a low correlation. By mixing these assets, we can reduce the overall volatility of our portfolio, regardless of how the individual investments are performing.

The risk-return relationship of investments typically results in lower-risk investments producing lower returns and higher-risk investments producing higher returns. A bank savings account has essentially no risk since our money is insured by the FDIC. Therefore, the return on investment (interest) that we earn from these accounts tends to be very low. On the other hand, our investments in stocks, bonds, and mutual funds are not insured, and they typically provide a greater return on investment over the long term, but there is no guarantee.

Our investment portfolio should consist of a diversified mix of index funds in stocks and bonds that are divided based on our risk-tolerance (comfort level), expected return, and long-term investment strategy.

Speculating is a high-risk, short-term strategy that seeks to profit from price increases resulting from company events or economic factors. Since buying and selling usually incur transaction fees, the profit made from speculating is reduced by these costs. The tech-stock bubble of the 1990s is a glaring example of speculation taken to the extreme. If we want to have a little fun speculating, we should use a small, segregated portion of our investments that we can afford to lose.

Chapter Ten

Asset Allocation

A typical well-diversified and risk-adjusted portfolio of investments would contain some bonds and some stocks. The bond portion would consist of bonds with certain maturities, and the stock portion would be made up of various segments of the market to gain broad exposure, while reducing risk (the risk associated with stocks that tend to move in the same direction). There are a variety of recommendations for how our investments should be divided, and most use our age to form at least some of the basis for the allocation. Age is used because there will be market downturns from time to time, and younger investors simply have more time for the market to recover when they experience a loss. For them, the allocation to stock is typically higher.

As an example, let's say that the stock market experiences a decline of 20 percent in value (let's say from 100 to 80). The market would have to increase by 25 percent in order to recover the loss (80 x 25% = 20), and this could take several years. A young investor can wait through these periods and continue to build wealth. As we approach retirement age, we are more interested in preserving our savings than we are in building more. Our personal asset allocation is somewhere between aggressive investments in stocks, and trading-off returns in order to protect our savings by investing in bonds.

In a previous chapter, we discussed the risk-return relationships and volatilities associated with different investments. We also saw that diversification within our investment portfolio can offset some of the overall risk. Our goal is to take advantage of the potentially higher returns of the stock market, while protecting a portion of our investment with assets that are less volatile, and diversifying our investments to offset market trends.

Shown below is a simplified portfolio with a 60 percent allocation to stock and a 40 percent allocation to bonds. The stock portion is divided (diversified) into domestic and foreign stocks, and the bond portion is in intermediate-term, highly rated (low risk) bonds. The Total Stock Market Index Fund contains all the US stocks, which provides the broadest domestic market exposure possible. The Total International Stock Index Fund contains all foreign stocks, and the Intermediate-Term Bond Fund contains over one thousand bonds with an average maturity of about seven years.

Simplified Allocation Strategy

Fund Description/Name	Asset Allocation
Total Stock Market Index Fund	45%
Total International Stock Index Fund	15%
Inter-Term Bond Market Index Fund	40%
	100%

The allocation could be more or less heavily weighted toward stocks, depending on our preferences. As a point of reference, the ten-year average returns for these funds are shown below with their risk ratings, ranging from one (the lowest risk) to five (the highest risk). Notice the relationship between the average returns and the risk ratings. As we'll discuss later, we develop our personal asset allocation based on this relationship.

Simplified Allocation Risk-Return

Fund Description/Name	10 Year Average	Risk Rating
Total Stock Market Index Fund	9.31%	4
Total International Stock Index Fund	10.62%	5
Inter-Term Bond Market Index Fund	6.09%	2

Source: Vanguard Group, Inc.

Further Diversification

If we want to increase the allocation of a specific area of the market, we can further diversify within the asset classes or market segments. For instance, we could split the total US stock market into large-cap, mid-cap, and small-cap stocks and then increase the investment in one or more. We could also split our foreign investments into European, Asian, and South American stocks (or many others), or into developed and emerging foreign countries and change the allocation.

In the simplified portfolio above, the Total Stock Market Fund contains mid-cap stocks in the same proportion as the overall stock market. If we wanted greater exposure to mid-cap stocks, we might add a mid-cap stock index fund to our investments. This will change the asset allocation for our portfolio, because there are now two funds containing mid-cap stocks. To determine the allocation to mid-cap stock, we would need to add the two investments together.

To show this in more detail, we'll look at the asset categories and allocations within the funds in the simplified strategy above. This information is readily available on fund websites. Below is the 2012 capitalization makeup of the Vanguard Total US Stock Market Index (ticker symbol VTSMX). The percentages closely match the market capitalization of the total US stock market.

Total US Stock Market Index Fund

Capitalization Composition

Large-Cap Stock	72%
Mid-Cap Stock	19%
Small-Cap Stock	9%

Source: The Vanguard Group, Inc.

Below is the 2012 capitalization make-up of the Vanguard Total International Stock Index Fund, which is their FTSE All-World ex-US Index Fund (VFWIX). This is made up of an asset mix of large- and mid-cap stocks. The fund does not contain any foreign small-cap stocks.

FTSE All-World ex-US Index Fund

Capitalization Composition

Foreign Large-Cap Stock	88%
Foreign Mid-Cap Stock	12%
Foreign Small-Cap Stock	0%

Source: The Vanguard Group, Inc.

To invest in certain foreign countries and not others, we could invest in specific foreign country funds. A quick review of the continent/country composition of the FTSE All-World ex-US Index Fund (shown below) would tell us which countries are already in the fund in our simplified allocation. (This composition is broken down further on the next page).

FTSE All-World ex-US Index Fund

Continent/Country Composition

Americas	13%
Greater Europe	48%
Greater Asia	39%

FTSE All-World ex-US Index Fund
Continent/Country Composition (Details)

<u>Americas</u>	<u>13%</u>
North America	8%
Latin America	5%
<u>Greater Europe</u>	<u>48%</u>
United Kingdom	14%
Europe	31%
Africa/Middle East	3%
<u>Greater Asia</u>	<u>39%</u>
Japan	13%
Australasia*	7%
Asia	19%

Source: The Vanguard Group, Inc.

*Australasia includes Australia, New Zealand, and other South Pacific islands.

Foreign stocks are usually divided into developed- and emerging-market categories. Emerging markets are foreign economies that are becoming industrialized, as opposed to established major-market economies. Emerging markets have the potential to grow very quickly, but also tend to be extremely volatile.

If we wanted to be invested in foreign emerging market stock, a little research would show that the international fund in the simplified allocation is already invested in that market segment.

FTSE All-World ex-US Index Fund (VFWIX) Market Classification

Developed Markets Stock	82%
Emerging Markets Stock	18%

Source: The Vanguard Group, Inc.

The intermediate-term bond fund in the simplified allocation contains bonds with an average maturity of about seven years. Short-term and long-term bond index funds could be added to the portfolio for further diversification and to invest in those maturities as well. If we're considering adding other bond maturities, it might pay to consider the Total Bond Market Index Fund (VBMFX), which includes all of the bond maturities as shown below.

Vanguard Total Bond Market Index Fund

Maturity Composition

Maturity	Percentage
Under 1 year	1.9
1 – 3 years	25.4
3 - 5 years	26.3
5 – 10 years	32.5
10 – 20 years	3.9
20 – 30 years	9.6
Over 30 years	0.4

Source: The Vanguard Group, Inc.

When we discussed bonds earlier, we focused on short-, intermediate-, and long-term bonds. This is because our discussion focused on the basic bond investment categories and strategies associated with most bond funds and investor preferences. As you can see from the list of maturities above, there are other options.

There are many different kinds of bonds and many different terms. A full discussion would require a separate book, and if you're interested in more information about bonds and bond investing, there's a website that I recommend at investinginbonds.com, which is run by a non-profit organization dedicated to providing everything you might ever want to know about bonds and the bond markets.

As far as performance or return on investment is concerned, the different bond maturities typically provide different returns. The one-year returns for index funds made up of the three bond maturities we discussed and for the total bond market index are shown below. The short- and long-term indexes tend to react more to changes in interest rates and inflation than the intermediate-term. This is why intermediate-term bond funds are popular with investors. We can't predict future performance, but past performance helps us understand how investments tend to react in certain economic conditions.

Bond Index Fund One Year Returns

Bond Index Fund	2012 Returns
Short-Term Bond Index Fund	1.70%
Inter-Term Bond Index Fund	6.60%
Long-Term Bond Index Fund	9.26%
Total Bond Market Index Fund	3.71%

Source: The Vanguard Group, Inc.

When we consider further diversification, it's important to be aware of what is already contained in the funds in our investment portfolio, or we could unknowingly change our investment asset allocation and increase risk. There are many mutual funds, including investments in specific portions of the market like value and growth stocks, or sectors like utilities, energy, or health care. But with fewer funds, our investments are more manageable and tend to produce the same or better returns.

If we want to invest more aggressively, we can easily modify our allocation strategy by increasing the stock portion of our investment. The simplified asset allocation we have been considering is invested in 60 percent stock, and 40 percent bonds. We could change this allocation to be more aggressive by increasing the stock portion to 70 percent. Later we'll look at funds that change with our age, and we can gain additional insight into some recommended asset allocations. This will give us something with which to compare our desired strategy.

Sample Portfolio Composition

To show further diversification, the three sample portfolios in this section (aggressive, moderate, and conservative) will contain separate funds for the domestic stock capitalizations (large-cap, mid-cap, and small-cap), as well as separate funds for foreign developed countries and emerging markets. A column for dollar amounts has been added to show the investment values.

The first example below is an aggressive investment portfolio of $100,000 made up of 80 percent stock and 20 percent bonds. The stock portion has an equal allocation to large-, mid-, and small-cap stocks. In addition, the foreign stock portion is 26 percent of the portfolio, and the intermediate-bond fund is only 20 percent of the investments.

Aggressive Portfolio Invested in 80% Stock and 20% Bonds

Asset	Percent of Portfolio	Amount
Bond Index Funds		
Inter-Term Bond Index	20%	$20,000
Stock Index Funds		
US Large-Cap Stock Index	18%	$18,000
US Mid-Cap Stock Index	18%	$18,000
US Small-Cap Stock Index	18%	$18,000
Foreign Developed Markets	18%	$18,000
Foreign Emerging Markets	8%	$8,000
	100%	$100,000

The allocation above with equal amounts to the three domestic stock funds differs significantly from the total US stock market fund in earlier examples. This allocation increases the amount of risk since mid-cap and small-cap stocks tend to be more volatile than larger stocks. The table below compares the stock capitalization allocations of the aggressive portfolio and the Vanguard Total US Stock Market Index Fund (VTSMX). The percentages compare just the stock portions.

Market Capitalization	VTSMX	Aggressive Portfolio
Large-Cap Stock	72%	33%
Mid-Cap Stock	19%	33%
Small-Cap Stock	9%	33%

Source: Vanguard Group, Inc.

In the moderate portfolio below, the bond allocation has been increased and the small-cap and foreign stock investments have been decreased. This allocation removes some of the volatility associated with those types of stocks and adds the stability of an increased bond investment. A $300,000 investment is used for the dollar amounts.

Moderate Portfolio Invested in 65% Stock and 35% Bonds

Asset	Percent of Portfolio	Amount
Bond Index Funds		
Inter-Term Bond Index	35%	$105,000
Stock Index Funds		
US Large-Cap Stock Index	18%	$54,000
US Mid-Cap Stock Index	18%	$54,000
US Small-Cap Stock Index	10%	$30,000
Foreign Developed Markets	12%	$36,000
Emerging Markets (Foreign)	7%	$21,000
	100%	$300,000

The conservative portfolio below ($1 million) increases the bond allocation further and reduces the mid-cap, small-cap, and foreign stock allocations. The US large-cap allocation has been increased and the foreign emerging market stocks have been removed to reduce risk.

Conservative Portfolio Invested in 50% Stock and 50% Bonds

Asset	Percent of Portfolio	Amount
Bond Index Funds		
Inter-Term Bond Index	50%	$500,000
Stock Index Funds		
US Large-Cap Stock Index	25%	$250,000
US Mid-Cap Stock Index	12%	$120,000
US Small-Cap Stock Index	8%	$80,000
Foreign Developed Markets	5%	$50,000
Emerging Markets (Foreign)	0%	$0
	100%	$1,000,000

When we compare the expected returns for the three portfolios (table below), we see the significant impact of the higher stock allocations over the long term. The table was calculated using 2012 average returns, and it assumed a $10,000 starting balance, no additional deposits, and all returns reinvested.

Sample Portfolio Hypothetical Returns ($10,000 starting balance)

Portfolio	5 Years	10 Years	20 Years	30 Years
Conservative	$16,927	$28,651	$82,088	$235,192
Moderate	$18,262	$33,350	$111,220	$370,914
Aggressive	$19,680	$38,731	$150,006	$580,985

The graph below shows the hypothetical growth of $10,000 invested in each of the three portfolios using Vanguard index funds as the assets.

Again, there are no additional deposits considered and returns are assumed to be reinvested.

Figure 10.1   Sample Portfolio Hypothetical Growth of $10,000

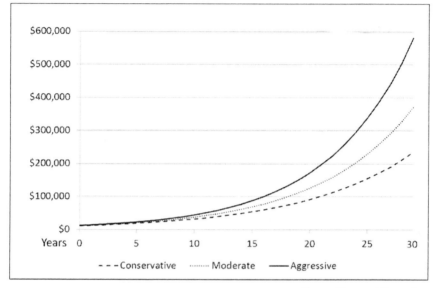

Source: Vanguard Group, Inc.

Value and Growth Stock Funds

As another option for diversification, stocks can also be separated into value and growth categories. *Value stocks* are stocks of companies with low expected growth, but they pay dividend income (they provide value). A mutual fund focused on dividend income would be invested in value stocks. *Growth stocks* are stocks of smaller companies with large growth potential. They don't typically pay dividends because they re-invest their earnings in research and development (to keep growing). Investors in growth stock funds are hoping for above-average increases in stock price (capital growth). Most of the funds in our examples would be considered *blend* funds meaning they contain both value and growth stocks.

Target Date Funds

Many people prefer to set their investment strategy on autopilot and take advantage of funds that change their asset allocation over time. The fund's asset composition is based on a recommended strategy that changes as a fixed date (usually retirement age) approaches. These mutual funds are called target date funds, and they reallocate their asset allocations based on the number of years until the target or retirement date. The asset allocations and diversification are within the one fund, so we simply invest in a single mutual fund, and the fund handles the rest.

The target retirement date is typically part of the name of the fund, so if I'm planning to retire in the year 2045, then a 2045 Target Date Fund would be an appropriate option. The fund would have an asset allocation that is more aggressive now and slowly becomes more conservative as 2045 approaches.

The table below shows the investment composition and allocation strategy of the Vanguard Target Retirement 2045 Fund (VTIVX). Notice how the asset allocation changes as the target (retirement) date approaches. Since we wouldn't withdraw everything from the account at retirement, there are also allocations beyond the target date.

Vanguard Target Retirement 2045 Fund Asset Composition

Asset	Percentage of Portfolio								
Cash	0%	0%	0%	0%	0%	0%	0%	4%	5%
Total Bond Market	10%	10%	17%	25%	33%	40%	40%	43%	45%
Inflation Protected Bonds	0%	0%	0%	0%	0%	0%	10%	17%	20%
Int'l Stock	27%	27%	25%	23%	20%	18%	15%	11%	9%
US Stock	63%	63%	58%	53%	47%	42%	35%	25%	21%
Years until Retirement	30	25	20	15	10	5	Retire	+5	+10

Source: The Vanguard Group, Inc.

Many target date funds, including those in employer-sponsored 401(k) accounts, have fees associated with them, and their portfolios often contain other funds that also have fees. These costs can reduce the return on investment, so review the prospectus to understand the costs associated with a target date fund before investing. As a point of reference, the expense ratio for the Vanguard fund above is just 0.18 percent as of January 2013.

Chapter Summary

Our asset allocation strategy is developed based on our personal risk-and-return preferences. Historically, certain assets tend to produce greater returns but are accompanied by greater volatility and risk. We dampen the volatility of our portfolio as a whole through diversification and by mixing various assets that tend to perform differently in response to economic changes. Younger investors tend to allocate a larger percentage of their portfolios to stocks since they have more time in life to recover from an extended market downturn. Older investors tend to allocate a larger portion of their investments to bonds in order to protect their savings. Target date funds follow this asset allocation strategy and automatically adjust the allocations over time.

We don't have to complicate our investments by having a large number of funds in our portfolio. We should consider what each additional asset provides in terms of risk and return and research the compositions of the funds already in the portfolio. The simplified allocation strategy in this chapter includes index mutual funds invested in intermediate-term bonds, the entire US stock market, and the entire foreign market (repeated below). These funds cover a very broad range of investments.

At one end of the spectrum, there are thousands of different funds made up of various slices of the market that we can use to create our own diverse portfolio, and at the other end there are all-in-one funds like target date funds or Vanguard's Life Strategy Growth Fund (VASGX) that put our investments on autopilot. Whichever strategy you choose, I recommend keeping it simple.

Simplified Allocation Strategy

Fund Description/Name	Asset Allocation
Total Stock Market Index Fund	45%
Total International Stock Index Fund	15%
Inter-Term Bond Market Index Fund	40%
	100%

If it still seems too complex, a mutual fund company or good financial advisor can provide professional counseling and recommend specific investments and asset allocations. If you have questions or concerns, seek professional advice and always make sure that you fully understand an investment before you commit any of your money.

Chapter Eleven

Building a Portfolio

In the last chapter, we looked at developing the asset allocation for our long-term savings plan. If we have a large sum of money saved, we can select our funds and make deposits in line with the allocations in the plan. If not, it might seem like our plan was a waste of time since most mutual funds require a $3,000 minimum investment (some require more), and we're limited by the amount of money that we have available to invest.

We could wait until we save a large amount in regular savings and then form a plan for investing, but it is possible to begin our long-term savings plan and invest with a limited amount of money. To do this, we use our asset allocation (portfolio investment) strategy, set an investment goal in dollars for our initial portfolio, and build toward our final portfolio goal a little at a time.

Our portfolio will consist of our asset allocation strategy (mix of stocks and bonds), and the funds that we select will act as placeholders until we have the money to invest. Let's look at two examples.

For the first example, assume that we've been saving for a while and have accumulated $10,000 to invest. We've established a strategy that includes an asset allocation of 30 percent invested in bonds and 70 percent invested in stocks. The bond portion will be diversified across the entire bond market (short-, intermediate-, and long-term), and the stock portion will be diversified across all US stocks (large-cap, mid-cap, and small-cap). We open an account with a mutual fund company, invest in the two funds, and we have a well-diversified investment portfolio. We really don't need to do any more.

Sample Initial Portfolio—$10,000

Asset	Portfolio	Percent of Amount
Total Bond Market Index Fund	30%	$3,000
Total Stock Market Index Fund	70%	$7,000
		$10,000

Since we accumulated the $10,000 in savings first (which could have taken a few years), we missed out on the returns that we could have earned from this portfolio had we started sooner. In 2012 alone, the Total Bond Market Index returned about 4 percent and the Total Stock Market Index returned about 16 percent. If we had made these investments in the beginning of the year, the value of our portfolio at the end of the year would have been $11,240 as shown below.

Asset Return on Investment 2012

Total Bond Market Index Return	$3,000 x 4% = $120
Total Stock Market Index Return	$7,000 x 16% = $1,120
Total Portfolio Return	$1,240

Portfolio Balance Change in Value 2012

Total Bond Market Index Balance	$3,000 + $120 = $3,120
Total Stock Market Index Balance	$7,000 + $1,120 = $8,120
Total Portfolio Balance	$11,240

The sample portfolio above was invested using the planned asset allocation strategy from the start. To maintain the same allocation, any additional investments would be made in the same proportions as the initial deposit unless returns have significantly changed the allocation. In the example, the 2012 returns would have changed the value of the investments. The stock portion would have grown by a much larger amount, which in turn would have made a slight change to the allocation for the portfolio as shown below. Over time, the difference in returns may cause the allocation percentages to stray too far from our plan. We'll cover this in more detail later in this section.

Portfolio Allocation as a Result of 2012 Returns

Asset	Value	Allocation
Total Bond Market Index Fund	$3,120	28%
Total Stock Market Index Fund	$8,120	72%
Total Bond Market Index Fund	$11,240	100%

The first example started with a $10,000 investment, but as I mentioned, we can start with a smaller amount, and work toward our goal one investment (deposit) at a time. For the second example, we'll start by determining the asset allocation for our *future* portfolio. In this case, we'll use an asset allocation of 55 percent in stocks and 45 percent in bonds. The stock portion will be 40 percent US stock and 15 percent international stock, and the bond investment will be in intermediate-term bonds.

Future Portfolio Asset Allocation

Asset	Asset Allocation
Total US Stock Market Index Fund	40%
Total International Stock Index Fund	15%
Inter-Term Bond Index Fund	45%
	100%

We set our first goal for the portfolio balance at $20,000, which we know we won't reach until sometime in the future. We use this goal for the balance to determine the individual goals in dollars that we'll be working toward for each fund. This is shown in the asset goal column in the table below. This column helps us plan our future deposits and is calculated using the asset allocation percentage and the $20,000 future goal for the portfolio.

For instance, the bond allocation will be 45 percent, so the asset goal for bonds is 45 percent of $20,000 which is $9,000. The asset goal amounts act as placeholders until we have the money needed to make those investments. Our first investment is a deposit of $3,000 into a Total US Stock Market Index Fund to gain exposure to the whole market. The initial portfolio plan and current balance after the $3,000 deposit are shown below.

Future Portfolio–Goal $20,000

Asset	Asset Allocation	Asset Goal	Actual Balance
Total US Stock Market Index Fund	40%	$8,000	**$3,000**
Total International Stock Index Fund	15%	$3,000	$0
Inter-Term Bond Index Fund	45%	$9,000	$0
		$20,000	**$3,000**

Although the portfolio is only invested in stocks initially, the total US stock market is very broad, and we plan our next deposit to further diversify and gain exposure to the bond market. We should also note that the investment made in the stock fund will be earning a return on investment while we're saving for the next deposit. As we accumulate savings to make future deposits, our previous investments are earning a return on our investment.

When we have another $3,000 to invest, the next investment will be made in the Intermediate-Term Bond Fund as shown in the table below.

Future Portfolio — Goal $20,000

Asset	Asset Allocation	Asset Goal	Actual Balance
Total US Stock Market Index Fund	40%	$8,000	$3,000
Total International Stock Index Fund	15%	$3,000	$0
Inter-Term Bond Index Fund	45%	$9,000	**$3,000**
		$20,000	**$6,000**

The next two deposits would be handled the same way. The first would be deposited to the Total US Stock Fund, and the second would increase the bond investment. The updated portfolio is shown below.

Future Portfolio–Goal $20,000

Asset	Asset Allocation	Asset Goal	Actual Balance
Total US Stock Market Index Fund	40%	$8,000	**$6,000**
Total International Stock Index Fund	15%	$3,000	$0
Inter-Term Bond Index Fund	45%	$9,000	**$6,000**
		$20,000	**$12,000**

Our next deposit could be made into the international stock fund or the bond fund. Whichever we chose, the deposit after that would go to the other, and after the next two deposits the portfolio balance would be near the initial goal of $20,000 (shown below).

Future Portfolio–Goal $20,000

Asset	Asset Allocation	Asset Goal	Actual Balance
Total US Stock Market Index Fund	40%	$8,000	$6,000
Total International Stock Index Fund	15%	$3,000	**$3,000**
Inter-Term Bond Index Fund	45%	$9,000	**$9,000**
		$20,000	**$18,000**

Now that the portfolio balance is approaching our $20,000 goal, we increase the overall goal for the portfolio and determine the new asset goal amounts for the center column. The asset allocation column will stay the same because we're maintaining the same asset allocation.

For the example, the portfolio goal has been changed to $30,000, and the asset goals have been recalculated below. These new amounts will be guiding our future investment deposits.

Future Portfolio–Goal $30,000

Asset	Asset Allocation	Asset Goal	Actual Balance
Total US Stock Market Index Fund	40%	$12,000	$6,000
Total International Stock Index Fund	15%	$4,500	$3,000
Inter-Term Bond Index Fund	45%	$13,500	$9,000
		$30,000	$18,000

These steps can be continued indefinitely as we accumulate savings and make deposits. Each time that the balance approaches our goal, we simply increase the portfolio goal and update the asset goal column. This helps to maintain our asset allocation strategy, but as we'll see later, our return on investment will have an effect on the balances that we may need to correct. But first, we'll review determining the return on investment for a diversified portfolio.

Determining Portfolio Return

Most investment companies provide quarterly and annual statements that list individual investment returns and account returns. If our investments are in a single account with a single company, then the one statement could provide the return-on-investment information. If not, then we can calculate the total return using the starting and ending balances for the accounts. The complexity of the calculation will depend on the complexity of the portfolio and whether or not we made any deposits or withdrawals during the time period. We'll look at both situations individually.

For the first example, we'll use a $10,000 portfolio with an allocation of 70 percent to stock and 30 percent to bonds. We'll assume that one year has passed and that the balances for the beginning and end of the year are as shown below.

Portfolio Assets	Beginning Balance	End of Year Balance
Total Stock Market Index Fund	$7,000	$8,120
Total Bond Market Index Fund	$3,000	$3,120
Total Amount	$10,000	$11,240

First, we first determine the change in the total account balance.

[Ending Balance – Starting Balance = Change in Balance]

$11,240 - $10,000 = $1,240

Next, we divide the change in the balance by the starting balance to determine the total return. The portfolio as a whole returned 12.4 percent for the period.

[Change in Balance / Starting Balance = Return]

$1,240 / $10,000 = 0.124, which is 12.4%

To see how the individual assets performed, we use a similar calculation. We first determine the change in the individual asset balance (the difference between the starting and ending balances) and divide by the starting balance of the asset.

[Ending Balance – Starting Balance = Change in Balance]

Stock Market Index: $8,120 - $7,000 = $1,120

Bond Market Index: $3,120 - $3,000 = $120

[Change in Balance / Starting Balance = Return]

Stock Market Index Fund: $1,120 / $7,000 = 0.16, which is 16%

Bond Market Index Fund: $120 / $3,000 = 0.04, which is 4%

The return for the Total Stock Market Fund was 16 percent, and the return for the Total Bond Market Fund was 4 percent, yet our portfolio returned 12.4 percent as a whole. This shows the greater influence of the stock portion of the portfolio on the overall return. The portfolio is said to be more heavily weighted toward stocks, since stocks make up a greater portion (70 percent) of the portfolio.

This is important to remember, especially when we consider losses. If the stock portion experienced a loss, it could outweigh a gain in bonds. As an example, the table below shows the portfolio values if the stock fund had lost 4 percent while the bond fund experienced a 4 percent gain. The 4 percent loss in the stock fund would more than offset the 4 percent gain in the bond fund, causing the portfolio as a whole to experience a 1.6 percent loss as shown below.

Asset	Starting Balance	Ending Balance	Change
Total Stock Market Index Fund	$7,000	$6,720	- $280
Total Bond Market Index Fund	$3,000	$3,120	$120
Portfolio	$10,000	$9,840	- $160

Total Bond Market Fund Return: $120 / $3,000 = 0.04, or 4%

Total Stock Market Fund Return: - $280 / $7,000 = -0.04, or -4%

Portfolio Return: - $160 / $10,000 = -0.016, or -1.6%

If our portfolio contains more funds, the calculations become more complicated. In addition, if we make deposits or withdrawals during the year, then we need to be sure to account for those in our return calculation.

Handling Deposits and Withdrawals

When we're making deposits and withdrawals with investment accounts, those transactions need to be removed from the balance in order to calculate an accurate return-on-investment value for the portfolio. For example, if we started the year with $10,000 in our account, deposited $5,400 during the year, and ended the year with an account balance of $16,518, the return on investment for the portfolio would be skewed by the deposit.

To determine the return on investment, we need to adjust for the $5,400 deposit before calculating the return. There are several ways to do this, and each one makes a different assumption. We'll review each method to see how they differ and to compare their accuracy.

The first method removes the deposit from the calculation and disregards any effect that it may have had on the return on investment. The deposit is excluded by subtracting it from the change in balance as shown below. The result is an estimated 11.2 percent return on investment.

Return Excluding the Deposit

Portfolio Ending Balance	$16,518
Portfolio Starting Balance	- $10,000
Change in Balance	$6,518
Subtract the Deposit	- $5,400
Return on Investment	$1,118

Portfolio Return as a Percentage = $1,118 / $10,000 = 11.2%

The calculations above assume that all of the returns were earned by the starting balance, and this would be true if the deposit was made at the end of the year when it could no longer affect returns. If the deposit was made early in the year, then it would have been part of the total balance that earned the return on investment. Let's compare this estimated return on investment to some other methods.

A second method for calculating the return includes the deposit in the return calculation for the year, by adding it to the starting balance. This method assumes that all of the returns for the year were earned by the higher balance (which includes the deposit). If the deposit was made in January, then adding it to the starting balance might be reasonable. If not, then we're making a poor assumption.

Using this method, the calculations (shown below) result in a 7.3 percent return on investment for the portfolio. This is very different from the 11.2 percent return previously calculated.

Return Including the Deposit in the Starting Balance

[Starting Balance + Deposit = Modified Starting Balance]

$10,000 + $5,400 = $15,400

Portfolio Ending Balance	$16,518
Modified Starting Balance	- $15,400
Change in Balance	$1,118

Portfolio return as a percentage = $1,118 / $15,400 = 7.3%

Since a deposit or a withdrawal could be made at the beginning of the year (when it would affect the balance over the entire period), toward the end of the year (when it would have a smaller affect), or throughout the year (like dollar-cost averaging), there is another method to calculate the return that spreads the change caused by the deposit.

With this method, half of the deposit amount is added to the beginning balance, and half is subtracted from the ending balance (shown below). This would be reversed in the case of a withdrawal.

Spreading the Deposit

Portfolio Ending Balance	$16,518
Minus Half the Deposit	- $2,700
Modified Ending Balance	$13,818

Portfolio Starting Balance	$10,000
Plus Half the Deposit	+ $2,700
Modified Starting Balance	$12,700

Next, we determine the difference between the modified starting and ending balances and use the modified starting balance to calculate the overall return. Again, the calculated return of 8.8 percent is quite different from the other two returns we calculated.

Spreading the Deposit, Modified Balances

Modified Ending Balance	$13,818
Modified Starting Balance	- $12,700
Return on Investment	$1,118

Portfolio Return as a Percentage = $1,118 / $12,700 = 8.8%

To test the results, assume that the deposit was actually made with monthly deposits of $450 (dollar-cost averaging). The table below shows the monthly returns and balances for an 8.64 percent return on investment resulting in a year-end balance of $16,518.11. This is very close to the estimated 8.8 percent return calculated above by spreading the deposit.

Monthly Balance and Return Data

8.64% Return and $450 Monthly Deposit

Month	Starting Monthly Balance	Monthly Return @ 8.64%	End of Month Balance
Jan.	$10,000.00	$72.00	$10,522.00
Feb.	$10,522.00	$75.76	$11,047.76
Mar.	$11,047.76	$79.54	$11,577.30
Apr.	$11,577.30	$83.36	$12,110.66
May	$12,110.66	$87.20	$12,647.86
Jun.	$12,647.86	$91.06	$13,188.92
Jul.	$13,188.92	$94.96	$13,733.88
Aug.	$13,733.88	$98.88	$14,282.76
Sep.	$14,282.76	$102.84	$14,835.60
Oct.	$14,835.60	$106.82	$15,392.42
Nov.	$15,392.42	$110.83	$15,953.24
Dec.	$15,953.24	$114.86	$16,518.11

The results from each of the methods are shown below for comparison. Calculating the return is simplified when investments are in the same account or with the same investment company, since most of them provide quarterly return statements with the information, but we can use these methods to obtain reasonable estimates when needed.

Results Comparison for the Three Methods

Method	Return
Subtract deposit from change in the balance	11.2%
Add deposit to the starting balance	7.3%
Spread the deposit	8.8%
Calculate each month's balance	8.64%

In the examples above, a deposit was being handled, but when we've made both deposits and withdrawals, this becomes a little more complicated. To simplify the calculations, we can combine deposits and withdrawals into a single amount called net additions/withdrawals.

Net Additions/Withdrawals

The net additions/withdrawals amount combines the deposits and withdrawals that were made during the period. For instance, if we deposited $5,400 into the account throughout the year and withdrew $1,000, then we could combine the transactions, and the net amount would be used in the return-on-investment calculations.

Calculating Net Additions and Withdrawals

Deposit amounts	+ $5,400
Withdrawal amounts	- $1,000
Net additions/withdrawals amount	$4,400

The methods covered previously for calculating the return treat a positive net additions/withdrawal amount as a deposit and a negative net additions/withdrawal amount as a withdrawal.

Rebalancing

Since stocks typically provide a higher return on investment than bonds, the stock portion of our investments will tend to grow faster. This causes the allocations to drift away from our asset allocation strategy. When the allocation percentages have drifted more than 5 percent, it's a good idea to realign them back to the original plan, or better put, rebalance the portfolio.

The best way to rebalance our portfolio is by making a deposit in the fund that has fallen behind. This eliminates any costs that might be incurred as a result of selling assets in one fund to buy assets in another fund. As an example, we'll use a $100,000 portfolio with an asset allocation of 60 percent stock and 40 percent bonds.

Sample Allocation 60% Stock and 40% Bonds

Asset	Current Balance	Percentage of Portfolio
Total Stock Market Index Fund	$60,000	60%
Total Bond Market Index Fund	$40,000	40%
Portfolio	$100,000	100%

If we assume that no deposits or withdrawals were made during the year and apply 2012 annual returns to the portfolio of 16 percent for stocks and 4 percent for bonds, the balances would change as a result of our market returns (shown below). Because of the higher returns from stocks and the larger portion of the portfolio being invested in stock, the stock portion of the portfolio would grow larger and change the asset allocation (right column).

To calculate the actual percentages for the assets, we divide each asset balance by the total balance for the portfolio. For instance, the calculation for the allocation of the stock fund is

$$\$69,600 / \$111,200 = 0.626 \text{ or about } 63\%.$$

Sample Allocation Balance Changes after 1 Year of Returns

Asset	Current Balance	Percentage of Portfolio
Total Stock Market Index Fund	$69,600	63%
Total Bond Market Index Fund	$41,600	37%
Portfolio	$111,200	100%

If the same return on investment occurred for a second year, the balances and asset allocation percentages would change again (shown below).

Sample Allocation Changes after 2 Years of Returns

Asset	Current Balance	Percentage of Portfolio
Total Stock Market Index Fund	$80,736	65%
Total Bond Market Index Fund	$43,264	35%
Portfolio	$124,000	100%

The planned allocation for the portfolio above was 60 percent stock and 40 percent bonds, but as a result of returns, the allocations are now 5 percent off from our plan. Increasing the amount in the bond fund by $10,560 would correct the allocation.

When we have additional funds or investments, changes to the allocation as a result of returns may not be as obvious. As an example, a column for the actual percentages has been added on the right for the sample portfolio below. We'll use this column to compare the actual allocation with the allocation goal. The planned allocation for the portfolio below is 55 percent stocks and 45 percent bonds. The portfolio balances have been selected at random for this example.

Portfolio–Goal $30,000 with Actual Allocations

Asset	Planned Allocation	Asset Goal	Portfolio Balance	Actual Allocation
Total US Stk Mrkt Index Fund	40%	$12,000	$10,332	42%
Total Int'l Stock Index Fund	15%	$4,500	$4,674	19%
Inter-Term Bond Index Fund	45%	$13,500	$9,594	39%
		$30,000	$24,600	100%

The actual allocation column shows that the asset mix has drifted from the plan for bonds. To determine the actual total stock allocation, the two actual stock percentages are added together.

Portfolio Stock Allocation   42% + 19% = 61%

Since the desired allocation for this portfolio is 55 percent stock and 45 percent bonds, we might consider rebalancing the allocation. We can rebalance by transferring money from one asset to another, or we can make an additional investment in the asset that has decreased in allocation. Since there may be costs associated with a transfer, when possible, a deposit is usually a better solution.

For the example, making a deposit of $1,000 to the US stock fund and $3,000 to the bond fund would bring the allocations much closer to the planned allocations as shown below.

Realigned Portfolio–Goal $30,000 with Actual Allocations

Asset	Planned Allocation	Asset Goal	Portfolio Balance	Actual Allocation
Total US Stk Mrkt Index Fund	40%	$12,000	**$11,332**	40%
Total Int'l Stock Index Fund	15%	$4,500	**$4,674**	16%
Inter-Term Bond Index Fund	45%	$13,500	**$12,594**	44%
		$30,000	**$28,600**	100%

Unless frequent deposits are being made that are affecting the allocation, checking them once a year should be sufficient. The whole point of our asset allocation is to diversify our investments to reduce risk and dampen the volatility of the market. Allowing the allocation to drift would defeat the purpose of having it in the first place. Once we've decided on our asset allocation strategy, it should be the same regardless of the size of the portfolio, unless we've decided to change it ourselves.

Changing Investment Strategy

Our investment strategy may change at times. We might want to invest more aggressively for a few years or maybe reduce risk as we get older by increasing our allocation to bonds. Whenever we change our investment strategy, the planned asset allocation for our investment portfolio will change.

To achieve the desired allocations, we first update the planned allocation column to the new strategy and then recalculate the asset goal dollar amounts column. Then we compare the actual allocation column on the far right to the planned allocation column, and the asset goals column to the portfolio balance column.

For example, let's assume that we've decided to change our allocation strategy and increase our stock allocation to 65 percent and decrease our bond allocation to 35 percent in the portfolio below. The savings goal for our portfolio is $40,000, which is used to calculate the new amounts for the asset goal column. Comparing the columns, we can see that future deposits would be made to the US Stock Market Index Fund, which has an actual allocation 10 percent below the new allocation strategy.

Adjusting Asset Allocation–Goal $40,000

Asset	Planned Allocation	Asset Goal	Portfolio Balance	Actual Allocation
Total US Stk Mrkt Index Fund	50%	$20,000	$11,332	40%
Total Int'l Stock Index Fund	15%	$6,000	$4,674	16%
Inter-Term Bond Index Fund	35%	$14,000	$12,594	44%
		$40,000	$28,600	100%

Making deposits to the US Stock Fund above will increase the percentage for that asset, while decreasing the percentages for the others. As an example, let's say that we made a $5,000 deposit to the stock fund. After the deposit, the updated actual allocation column below shows that the deposit adjusted the allocations in line with the new plan.

Adjusted Asset Allocation–Goal $40,000.00

Asset	Planned Allocation	Asset Goal	Portfolio Balance	Actual Allocation
Total US Stk Mrkt Index Fund	50%	$20,000	**$16,332**	49%
Total Int'l Stock Index Fund	15%	$6,000	$4,674	14%
Inter-Term Bond Index Fund	35%	$14,000	$12,594	37%
		$40,000	$33,600	

During short cycles of high volatility or during market lulls, we might be tempted to change strategies, but shifting strategies and changing allocations in reaction to market changes tends to work against us. As we get older, we might want to shift our asset allocation to more conservative investments, but in general, determining an asset allocation that fits our risk tolerance and return expectations and sticking with it, produces the best results.

Getting Started

Establishing an IRA account or investment portfolio has been made relatively easy by financial and mutual fund companies. We can establish an account on their website or request the appropriate forms through e-mail or phone. Once the account is established, we can make deposits to the account either through bank transfers, direct deposit, or sending them a check. If we're handling the portfolio ourselves, we should establish our planned asset allocation and determine the funds that we plan to invest in ahead of time. Then we simply work to our planned portfolio through additional deposits, monitor the returns, and maintain the asset allocation. Most fund companies provide asset allocation tools on their websites that compare our preferred (or planned) allocation to the investments in our account.

The goal is to get started and build our long-term savings a little at a time using a well-planned investment strategy that fits our risk tolerance and expected returns.

Chapter Summary

Before we build our portfolio (begin investing), we determine our asset allocation based on our tolerance for risk and expected return and select the funds that will make up our investments. If we don't have savings on hand to invest in all of the funds in our plan, we establish the amounts for our future portfolio and begin by investing in one of the funds and build the portfolio one step at a time.

We should monitor our investment balances and review the return on investment for the portfolio as a whole and the returns for the individual funds. The quarterly statements or account information on the company website may provide return data, or we can calculate the total return using the methods in this chapter.

If we've made deposits and withdrawals from investment accounts, those transactions need to be removed from the balance in order to calculate an accurate return-on-investment value for the portfolio. When we've made both deposits and withdrawals in a given year, we can combine the transactions into a single amount called net additions/withdrawals and use this amount in our calculations.

Over time, our deposits or the differences in investment returns may cause the allocation percentages to stray from our plan. Since a change in allocation also changes the risk-return relationship of the portfolio, we should realign the allocations by transferring between assets or directing future deposits to specific assets. The time and effort expended to establish our asset allocation is wasted if we allow it to drift over time.

Our investment preferences may change at various times throughout our lives. When we change our investment strategy, we also change the planned asset allocation for our portfolio. The difference between our new plan and our actual fund balances will indicate where future investments should be directed to achieve the new allocation. Whenever possible we should use new deposits to adjust the allocations to avoid any costs associated with selling and buying or transferring money from one fund to another.

When the market is going through a cycle of volatility, we should resist the temptation to change strategies because shifting strategies and changing allocations in reaction to the market tends to work against us, and is not in line with our long-term investment strategy. We'll discuss investing further in coming chapters.

Chapter Twelve

Survivorship Planning

Survivorship planning is an often overlooked area of personal finance or is limited to large obligations like a mortgage, and it doesn't consider the many smaller items that add up to large amounts of money. When we evaluate our life insurance needs, we should start by analyzing the ability of our dependents to continue financially without us beginning tomorrow, and then we should think about how we can minimize the financial impact of our sudden death. This analysis will include much more than the balance on our mortgage.

To accomplish survivorship planning thoroughly and accurately, we need to consider all current and future expenses and obligations as though we wouldn't be here. Since we wouldn't want our survivors to have to worry about where they were going to live, typically housing is the first consideration. There will either be a mortgage payment or rental costs, and they should be included in the evaluation. Next, we need to assess everyday living expenses, current debts and liabilities, any planned future expenses (like a child's college fund), and then account for our survivor's expenses in their retirement years. Finally, we compare this total to our current savings and investments and life insurance. This provides a thorough determination of the financial situation that we might leave behind.

Since the information is continually changing as we pay debts and eliminate obligations, this analysis should be performed annually or whenever a major financial change occurs.

Survivorship Planning

- survivor current expenses
- debts and current liabilities
- planned future expenses
- survivor retirement expenses
- savings and investments
- life insurance

Before we walk through survivorship, there are two numbers we should review because they tend to get a lot of attention: the first is net worth and the second is economic value. Each of these numbers has some merit as a point of reference in survivorship planning.

Net Worth

Our net worth is simply all of our assets minus all of our liabilities. This amount is sometimes used to determine credit-worthiness. It shows if we owe more money than the value of our assets and if we could pay off all of our debts by liquidating (selling) all of our assets. This isn't something we would normally do, but sometimes when we're applying for a loan, our net worth is used by the lender to assess our current financial situation.

Since net worth includes all assets (houses, cars, etc.) and we wouldn't want our survivor to have to sell them, net worth really shouldn't be used in survivorship planning. It's simply a picture of where we stand financially in terms of current assets and liabilities.

And a large asset like a second home would be considered part of our savings and investments.

Let's use a married couple as an example and determine their net worth by starting with a review of their assets. We'll assume that the couple owns a home worth $250,000, two cars worth $20,000 each, and they have savings and investments totaling $100,000. Even though the value of a house or car is an estimate, for the example, we'll assume that these amounts are the fair market values (what they could be sold for in a reasonable period of time). Any money owed on these assets will be accounted for in the liabilities portion of calculation. The amounts for the assets are added together to determine the couple's total asset amount (shown below).

Total Assets at Market Value

Home	$250,000
Two cars ($20,000 each)	$40,000
Savings/investments	$100,000
Total assets	$390,000

Next, we look at liabilities. We'll assume that they have a mortgage on the house with a principal balance of $195,000, one of the cars has a loan with an outstanding balance of $16,000, and they have a personal loan with a balance of $10,000. Any large credit card balances would be included here as well.

Total Liabilities

Mortgage	$195,000
Car loan	$16,000
Personal loan	$10,000
Total liabilities	$221,000

Their net worth is their current assets minus their current liabilities which is $169,000.

Net Worth

Total assets	$390,000
Total liabilities	-$221,000
Net worth	$169,000

In the example, the couple's net worth is a positive number, which means that the value of their assets is greater than their liabilities. Although this is better than a negative net worth, it really doesn't tell us that much. For instance, we don't know their spending and saving habits or what they're currently earning. It's a financial picture of today.

A number that's related to net worth called *recommended* net worth is determined by multiplying our age by our gross income and then dividing by ten. Recommended net worth is often compared to actual net worth, but again, this tells us very little about the couple's financial situation. The couple in the example above has a net worth of $169,000. If they earn a combined annual salary of $124,000 and they're both forty-two years old, then their recommended net worth would be $520,800 as shown below.

Recommended Net Worth

(Age x Gross income)/10 = Recommended net worth

(42 x $124,000.00) /10 = $520,800

A rising net worth indicates a positive financial trend, and a decreasing net worth could be a warning sign, especially if it's below the recommended net worth amount. Other than comparing these two numbers, they have little value. We don't use them in planning or analysis.

Economic Value

Our personal economic value is simply our future earnings potential. It's the total amount that we could earn between now and when we plan to stop working. We think about our annual income each year when we file income tax, but we don't often consider the total amount that we will earn in the future. Since we'll total all of our preretirement expenses for survivorship planning, our economic value can be an interesting number for evaluation because we can compare our total preretirement earnings with our total preretirement expenses. This can be valuable because we're always looking for discretionary income and ways to increase our savings.

Economic value is earnings potential, and we might think that we just multiply earnings times the number of years until retirement. The couple in the example earns $124,000 each year and they plan to retire twenty years from now, so the equation below might seem correct.

Presumed Economic Value

Income x Years of income = Economic value?

$124,000 x 20 = $2,480,000

The problem with this estimate is that it overlooks any increases in earnings that they might receive over the twenty year period that they'll be working before retirement. If they receive 3 percent pay increases each year, then the total amount, or economic value, will be very different.

Just like compound interest, the increases or raises are applied to the current income amount, which would be rising each year as a result of the increases in previous years. As an example, let's assume that they receive a 3 percent raise every year and calculate the change in income. The first year is shown below.

Calculating Economic Value (First Year)

Current income + (Current income x 3%) = Second year income

$124,000 + ($3,720) = $127,720

Their second year or new income is $127,720, and after the second year the raise is applied to their updated income amount (below).

Calculating Economic Value (Second Year)

New income + (New income x 3%) = Third year income

$127,720.00 + ($3,831.60) = $131,551.60

In our example, there are twenty years until retirement, so this increase would occur every year for nineteen years (nineteen years and not twenty because it begins at the end of the first year). If we continue with the calculations above for all 19 years (shown below) and add the earnings together, the total is $3,331,926.44. This is their earnings potential or personal economic value.

Income $124,000, over 20 Years, with a 3% Increase Each Year

Year	Income
1	$124,000.00
2	$127,720.00
3	$131,551.60
4	$135,498.15
5	$139,563.09
6	$143,749.99
7	$148,062.48
8	$152,504.36
9	$157,079.49
10	$161,791.87
11	$166,645.63

12	$171,645.00
13	$176,794.35
14	$182,098.18
15	$187,561.13
16	$193,187.96
17	$198,983.60
18	$204,953.11
19	$211,101.70
20	$217,434.75
Total	$3,331,926.44

Before we move on, notice the difference between the two numbers that we calculated. Simply taking current income times the number of years until retirement resulted in an estimate of $2,480,000. When we include expected increases in the income each year, the result is $3,331,926.44. The difference is $851,926.44. This is a large amount and will become more important as we continue the example.

If our raises are not consistent, we can use an average amount. For instance, if some years we receive 3 percent and other years 1 percent, then we could use 2 percent as an average. But we can't overlook raises, because the difference in total earnings could be very large like the example and because we apply inflation to expenses when we plan for survivorship, so increases in income (which typically coincide with inflation) will be very important.

So is $3,331,926.44 what the survivor in the example would need starting tomorrow? Not really … there's much more that we need to consider. Net worth and economic value are simply points of reference. The total cost associated with actually paying the expenses and debt obligations is the amount that we need to determine. This brings us to expenses and in-depth survivorship planning.

Survivorship

In survivorship planning, we're determining financial needs as though we're deceased and no longer earning income (or getting raises). The same way that we looked at income increasing over the years, we need to consider how expenses will change. Our expenses tend to coincide with our income (if we make more, we tend to spend more), but part of this is due to inflation and the fact that raises generally just keep up with increases in the cost of goods and services. Our survivorship plan needs to account for this annual increase in expenses. We can use current expenses as a starting point and apply inflation for the number of years that our survivor will need to pay them. From that point we can determine a total amount of expenses that our survivor can expect to pay through life expectancy, adjusted for inflation.

In addition to total expenses, we need to consider our current debt situation (liabilities), which would need to be paid by our survivor. Then, we need to consider the changes that will occur when our survivor reaches retirement age. Since these changes will be significant, our survivorship calculations will be divided into two sections: the time before and the time after our survivor's retirement date. There are several important reasons why this is done.

First, total preretirement expenses will change every month as expenses are paid and move into the past. We no longer need to prepare for them once they're paid and behind us. For instance, when we perform the analysis today, it will include next month's mortgage payment. If we perform another analysis a month from now, this payment would no longer be included, since it was paid. In addition, preretirement debt may increase or decrease. Whenever we reevaluate survivorship, these amounts will need to be updated so that current amounts are used in the calculations.

Second, preretirement expenses are used to calculate postretirement amounts, so segregating them into two calculations is necessary. Finally, there will be changes to both income and expenses for our survivor beginning on their retirement date. These changes will need to be included only from that point forward. Let's start with regular expenses.

Preretirement Expenses

First, we'll determine total expenses beginning tomorrow and ending on the survivor's planned retirement date. This is calculated using our current annual expense amount, and the same way that we applied raises to the income amount above, we'll apply inflation to the expenses. Using the couple in the example, their combined earnings are $124,000, they're both forty-two years old, and annual expenses are $75,000. They currently plan to retire twenty years from now when they're both sixty-two years old. The anticipated annual inflation rate we'll use is 2 percent, so each year expenses will increase by 2 percent, and in twenty years (at the planned retirement date) annual expenses will have increased from $75,000 to $109,260.84 due to inflation.

When we calculate the expense amounts for each of the years until the retirement year while applying inflation and add the annual amounts together, the result is $1,822,302.73 in total expenses. This is the total of all known expenses beginning tomorrow and ending with the survivor's retirement, adjusted for inflation over the time period.

Total inflation adjusted preretirement expenses $1,822,302.73

If the couple is planning any major purchases or a child's college expenses before retirement, then an estimate of those costs would be added to the total expense amount (this will be included later). But notice that we've exposed an opportunity. If the total amount for expenses between now and retirement is $1,822,302.73, and the couple's economic value (earnings potential) that we calculated in the previous section is $3,331,926.44, then potential income is far greater than expected expenses. This reveals an opportunity for the couple to increase their regular saving amount or pay down debt. We tend to look at income and expenses monthly, but there's a much larger picture that we should review periodically.

Economic Value and Preretirement Expenses Comparison

Economic value	$3,331,926
Preretirement expenses	-$1,822,303
Difference	$1,509,623

Postretirement Expenses

For the next step, we estimate the total expenses beyond the planned retirement date. To do this, we start with the expense amount calculated for the survivor's retirement year. Although this amount could change (a debt may be paid off between now and retirement), this is where people often short-change themselves in retirement planning. They estimate that their mortgage will be paid off or that they won't have a car loan. Think carefully when assuming that a debt will be eliminated before retirement. There will still be some type of housing expenses, and a new car might be needed later in life. Trim retirement expenses only after serious consideration. People are staying active longer into retirement, traveling more, and living longer than expected.

For the couple in the example, we'll assume that expenses have remained the same. As a starting point in the calculations, we use the inflation-adjusted expense amount for the final year of preretirement. We determined above that at retirement (twenty years from now), annual expenses for the couple would be $109,260.84 as a result of inflation.

Regular expenses (first year of retirement) $109,260.84

This is the starting point for annual expenses in retirement, which will end at life expectancy. If we assume a life expectancy of age ninety-five, then there will be thirty-three years (ages sixty-two to ninety-five) of expenses that will need to be paid by the survivor. When we calculate the annual expense amounts for each of these thirty-three years while applying a 2 percent rate of inflation and add them together, the total amount is $5,038,188.89. This is the total of all expenses from the retirement date to life expectancy, based on the expenses at retirement and adjusting for inflation.

Total inflation adjusted postretirement expenses $5,038,188.89

If the couple is expecting some type of retirement income like social security or a pension, the income would be subtracted from the expense amount as a total amount. In the case of a pension or annuity, the income amount will most likely be fixed (the same every year). Social security may receive a cost-of-living adjustment, meaning it may increase in some years, but there is no guarantee. The cost-of-living adjustment to social security is based on inflation and government approval, so we're safer considering pensions and social security as fixed income. This is why we total expenses and income separately for the retirement period. Expenses change every year, but income is a fixed amount.

If we were to simply subtract income from expenses each year in retirement before applying inflation, we would affect the income amount along with expenses. Doing this would assume that income would be rising with inflation, which is not the case. To adjust for income during retirement, we multiply the fixed income amount by the years of retirement (thirty-three years in the example), to determine the total income amount that will be received in retirement. Then we compare the total postretirement income and the total postretirement expenses to determine if there is a surplus or shortfall amount. To show why this is important, let's do the calculations both ways.

Part 1: Subtracting fixed income from expenses before applying inflation.

We'll assume that the couple is expecting $3,000 in monthly fixed income ($36,000 annually) in retirement, and we'll subtract the income from the expense amount before applying inflation. The "annual expenses at retirement" amount of $109,260.84 minus the "annual retirement income" of $36,000 will equal a "remaining retirement expense" amount of $73,260.84 for the first year.

Annual expenses at retirement	$109,260.84
Annual retirement income	-$36,000.00
Remaining retirement expense amount	$73,260.84

Now we apply 2 percent inflation to each year through life expectancy (thirty-three years) and add the annual amounts together. The result is a "postretirement expenses" total of $3,378,172.37 (adjusted for retirement income and inflation).

Postretirement expense total adjusted for fixed income $3,378,172.37

Part 2: Calculating the total expenses in retirement and total income in retirement separately, and applying inflation to only the expense portion.

Using this method, we first apply inflation to the retirement expense amount of $109,260.84 for thirty-three years and add the amounts together. Then we calculate the "total fixed income" amount received over thirty-three years and subtract this amount from the "total inflated expense" amount. When we calculate the expense amounts for each year using 2 percent inflation and add them together (as we did above), the total amount is $5,038,188.89.

Postretirement expense amount $5,038,188.89

Next we multiply the "postretirement fixed income" amount of $36,000 by thirty-three years, which is $1,188,000, and then subtract this from the "postretirement expense" total. The difference is the "remaining retirement expense" amount (apart from fixed income).

Postretirement inflation adjusted expense total	$5,038,188.89
Postretirement income total	-$1,188,000.00
Remaining retirement expense amount	$3,850,188.89

Postretirement remaining expense total $3,850,188.89

Previously, when we subtracted income from expenses prior to inflation, the total was $3,378,172.37, which overlooked $472,016.52 of expenses in retirement. This is why I recommend calculating them separately. A large amount of expenses could be easily overlooked.

Putting Them Together

To complete the analysis, we add the "preretirement expense" total (all expenses between tomorrow and retirement) to the "adjusted postretirement expense" total. The result is the "total inflation-adjusted expense" amount for the time period beginning tomorrow and ending at life expectancy for the survivor (including postretirement income).

Total Survivorship Expense Amount

Preretirement expense total	$1,822,302.73
(Income-adjusted) postretirement expense total	$3,850,188.89
Total survivorship expense amount	$5,672,491.62

Next, we need to include any debt that the couple has aside from their regular expenses and any future expenses that the couple might be planning like a child's college expenses. They have a mortgage, a car loan, and a personal loan, but payments for these debts were included in the monthly expenses, so adding them here would count them twice. We'll assume that the couple is planning to have children and want to set aside $200,000 for college expenses in a college fund. This amount is added here.

Total Expense Amount

Total survivorship expense amount	$5,672,491.62
College Fund Expense	$200,000.00
Total survivorship expense amount	$5,872,491.62

We've included all future expenses and postretirement income in the calculations, and we can now consider the couple's current savings and investments, which were $100,000 in the example. We don't apply growth to this amount for the same reason that we don't include our income: the money might be needed by our survivor starting tomorrow. Next we subtract current savings and investments from the total expense amount.

Total Expenses Adjusting for Current Savings and Investments

Total survivorship expense amount	$5,872,491.62
Current savings & investments	-$100,000.00
Shortfall	$5,772,491.62

The shortfall amount of $5,772,491.62, is the total amount of payable expenses for the survivor beginning tomorrow and ending at life expectancy with a 2 percent annual inflation rate applied, planned college expenses included, an adjustment for postretirement income, and taking into consideration current savings and investments.

So is $5,772,491.62 the amount of life insurance the couple should have? Not really, for two reasons: (1) Since both members of the couple work, the survivor may continue to work in some capacity. This would be used to offset the preretirement expense amount used in the equation.

(2) A life insurance check would be deposited or invested and would provide interest or a return on investment while annual withdrawals were made to pay expenses. To compensate for the return on investment of the life insurance amount, we use the savings longevity calculation covered in the chapter on retirement. This would determine a more exact amount based on the return on investment, inflation rate, and the amount of the annual withdrawals. For the purpose of this example, we can make a conservative estimate.

The annual expense amount needed immediately (tomorrow) by the survivor is $75,000, and we assumed a 2 percent inflation rate. The survivor would deposit the life insurance check, and to simplify the estimate, we can assume that it earns a 2 percent return on investment. The 2 percent return on investment would offset the effects of 2 percent inflation, and we can calculate an estimate for life insurance by multiplying the expense amount ($75,000) by the number of years (fifty-three) they would need to be paid. We then add $100,000 for the college fund, since there is already $100,000 in savings. The result is a life insurance amount of about $4 million, which is a reasonable estimate as long as the inflation rate is 2 percent or less, and the return on investment is at least 2 percent (which is conservative). The equations are shown below.

$75,000 x 53 Years = $3,975,000

$3,975,000 + $100,000 = $4,075,000

Estimated survivor life insurance protection $4,075,000

Life Insurance

There are basically three types of life insurance: term, whole life, and universal life. They differ slightly from company to company, but essentially term life insurance is coverage that is purchased for a certain period of time, whole life has a cash value that accumulates over the years, and universal life includes an investment portion. Due to the complexities of insurance products, it's important to understand the coverage, benefits, and shortcomings of each type. We should consider our individual circumstances, the coverage needed, and the cost of the insurance.

In the example above, as the couple increases their savings and debts are paid, they would need less insurance. If they lock themselves into a long-term $4 million policy, they could eventually be paying for insurance that they no longer need. Many employers offer reduced rates on insurance products for their employees, but very often these policies are only available while we're an active employee. The loss of employment, or retirement could terminate this insurance, so be sure to understand the provisions of the policy. For the couple in the example, a $4 million term life insurance policy would be sufficient, and as the years go by they can lower this amount.

Chapter Summary

We perform survivorship planning to ensure that our survivor could continue financially through life expectancy, in the event of our death. We evaluate the complete financial lifetime for our survivor, including all future expenses, current debts and financial obligations, savings and investments, retirement income, and the effects of inflation. Since many of the values change over time, survivorship plans should be updated annually or whenever a financial change occurs. The goal is to provide lifelong financial protection for our loved ones, in case we're not around.

Chapter Thirteen

Preparing for Retirement

Many people see retirement as a time when they will stop working and take an extended vacation, beginning at a certain age (the earlier the better) and ending with death. For others, it's a time to be more focused on contributing, sharing, and helping others with the skills and abilities accumulated over a lifetime. If we're prepared financially, we'll have the option to apply ourselves to efforts that are more personally fulfilling but perhaps don't pay as well as the career we're leaving behind or that don't provide any income. If we're not prepared financially, we can delay retirement or continue to work in some capacity. But regardless of our view of retirement, we know that when the time comes, there will be changes to our lifestyle and financial situation.

For many people, this transition is far into the future, and they have reservations about ever having enough saved to retire. For others, retirement is approaching, and there are doubts about how long their savings will last. In both cases, the issue is how much savings is needed to retire comfortably with some assurance that it will last.

For a younger person, there is no way of knowing what income or expenses will be twenty, thirty, or forty years in the future, but we can make some reasonable estimates and determine the amount of money needed to retire. This way, a savings plan and goal can be established. Without a specific and personal retirement savings goal, there is no way to form an achievable plan, make adjustments, or measure progress, and not much incentive to save.

The first step in determining the goal is to estimate a retirement expense amount, because all of our planning is affected by the expenses that we'll need to pay. Then we take into account all of the variables: the age retirement will begin, how much income there will be in retirement, and economic factors such as inflation and taxes. As we'll see, changing any of these can have a significant impact on the total savings required for retirement and how long it will last. Since we're dealing with the future, we'll have to make some assumptions, but they need to be realistic and conservative. Unrealistic assumptions made now can put us in a very bad position later in life when trying to make up for a financial shortfall is much more difficult if not impossible.

Looking Far into the Future

If we're just starting out in the working world, then we're in our early earning years. We hear that we should save as much as we can, but we're not really motivated to save, especially when we want or need something now. There isn't much incentive for us to make weekly sacrifices and accumulate $1 million in savings when we have plans like buying a house and starting a family.

How do we determine a realistic goal, form a plan, and then save according to the plan without feeling like we're cheating ourselves in our early years? The answer begins with first understanding the importance and extent of the situation. Once we understand why we're saving and how much is needed, we can develop a plan based on our current situation, work to the plan, and adjust the plan as a result of changes in our lives. If we determine the savings goal ourselves and have confidence in the numbers and decisions leading to the goal, then we're more inclined to work toward it. We'll have a retirement savings goal that we developed based on our own financial situation and plans for the future.

Since we can't see the future, there are some realistic assumptions that we'll have to make to develop our plan. First, we need to determine when retirement will begin, and since age sixty-five is fairly common, we can use that for our plan. Next, we'll determine our living expenses. We'll need a place to live, whether we're renting or own a house, so we'll have some amount of housing expenses. It's true that our mortgage might be paid off by then, but we don't know that for sure, and we'll still have property taxes, maintenance, and other home-owner expenses, or we'll be paying rent.

In addition to housing, we use a group of realistic expenses to determine an estimated monthly and annual retirement expense amount. Once we've compiled a comprehensive list of regular expenses, we adjust for the effects of inflation over the retirement period because the cost of products and services will rise over the years. When we total the annual expense amounts, we'll have a reasonable estimate of what we'll need to transition comfortably, even though we've made a few assumptions. To begin, let's look at retirement expenses.

Expenses in Retirement

It might seem logical that expenses in retirement would be lower than preretirement expenses, but millions of Americans are finding out that this isn't the case. When estimating an expense amount for retirement, we have to be careful not to short-change ourselves. It will be very difficult to increase our income if we run out of money in the middle of retirement. We need to consider every possible retirement expense in our planning now so that they're included in our savings goal amount. In retirement, we'll be living on a fixed income and withdrawing from our savings to pay expenses.

Below is a list of typical retirement expenses for reference. If you refer back to the expense list in the chapter on budgets, you'll find that the two lists are very similar. We will still have most of the same expenses that we have in our preretirement years. A few expenses (such as child care) may no longer apply, but other expenses will replace them.

Typical Retirement Expenses

<u>General Living</u>
food
sundries/toiletries
clothing/dry cleaning
phone/cell phone
cable TV/internet
drugs/medication
office visits/co-pay
dental/optical
health insurance
life insurance

<u>Housing</u>
mortgage/rent
insurance/taxes
association dues
home maintenance
heating/elec.
water/sewer
trash/garbage
grounds care
home security

<u>Transportation</u>
bus/cab fare
parking/tolls
fuel
auto insurance
maintenance
registration
auto loan

<u>Other Expenses</u>
charitable donations
pet care/vet/food/meds
hobbies/club dues
vacations/travel
gifts/parties/holidays
tax installments
loan payments

As you review the list, think carefully before excluding items. The retirement savings plan will be developed from this list, so items that are removed won't be included in future expenses. If we make any assumptions, they should be conservative because it's much better to reach retirement with a little extra money than to find ourselves retired without enough to pay expenses. For instance, I don't use "grounds care" now because I like to work outside. When I retire, this may prove difficult, especially when it comes to shoveling large snowfalls. We need to consider how life might be different at that time in our lives.

Once we've compiled a list of expenses, we can add realistic costs and determine a monthly and an annual retirement expense amount.

Monthly Retirement Expense Amounts

General Living	Monthly	Housing	Monthly
Food	$400	Mortgage/rent	$1,800
Sundries/toiletries	$200	Insurance/taxes	$0
Clothing/dry cleaning	$0	Association dues	$120
Phone/cell phone	$90	Home maintenance	$200
Cable TV/Internet	$90	Heating/electricity	$300
Drugs/medication	$120	Water/sewer	$40
Office visits/co-pay	$50	Trash/garbage	$100
Dental/optical	$50	Grounds care	$120
Health insurance	$1,000	Home security	$100
Life insurance	$100		
Total	$2,100	Total	$2,780

Transportation	Monthly	Other Expenses	Monthly
Bus/cab fare	$0	Charitable donations	$400
Parking/tolls	$20	Pet care/vet/food/meds	$0
Fuel	$150	Hobbies/club dues	$100
Auto insurance	$100	Vacations/travel	$200
Maintenance	$50	Gifts/parties/holidays	$50
Registration	$0	Tax installments	$0
Auto loan	$0	Loan payments	$0
Total	$320	Total	$750

For my grounds care expense, I apply an average cost that I know people are paying today for the service. We use today's costs even though we know they'll most likely be higher in the future, because we'll be applying inflation to the amounts.

Inflation

Inflation is often overlooked in retirement planning and can have a major impact on expenses due to the long period of time involved. For instance, if my monthly expenses today are $2,500 and the inflation rate is 2 percent, then next year the same expenses could cost $2,550. If inflation remains constant, then in twenty years the same monthly expenses will cost $3,714.87. This is extremely important for someone with a retirement date forty years from now and a life expectancy thirty years beyond retirement. They could experience seventy years of inflation through their lifetime.

Using the example table for retirement expenses above, the total monthly amount for all expense categories is $5,950, which is $71,400 annually as shown below. This number will change each year as retirement approaches and the amounts are recalculated.

Total Monthly Retirement Expenses

Expense Categories	Monthly
General living	$2,100
Housing	$2,780
Transportation	$320
Other expenses	$750
Total	$5,950

$5,950 x 12 months = $71,400

Because of inflation, the estimated annual expense amount above will change every year. The more time there is between now and retirement, the greater the increase in annual expenses.

The table below shows the long-term effects of inflation on the annual expense total in the example. Two things should immediately get our attention: the major impact of inflation over time and the mistake of not including inflation in retirement estimates. If the amounts seem unbelievable, remember that $26,000 was a fairly common price for a house fifty years ago.

The Effect of Inflation on Annual Expenses

	Total Years of Inflation				
Inflation Rate	50	55	60	65	70
0%	$71,400	$71,400	$71,400	$71,400	$71,400
1%	$116,264	$122,195	$128,428	$134,979	$141,864
2%	$188,411	$208,021	$229,672	$253,577	$279,969
3%	$303,894	$352,297	$408,408	$473,457	$548,866

Continuing with the example, there are two inflation adjustments that need to be made in order to segregate the amounts that we'll be using. The first applies to the time between now and our retirement date, and the second applies to the period between retirement and life expectancy. We separate the two inflation adjustments when we do retirement planning because the time period between now and retirement will decrease every year as we approach retirement. When we reevaluate the retirement savings plan in the future, this will lower the number of years that we apply inflation to that portion of the equation. The number of years after retirement will always stay the same (unless we change it intentionally), but the postretirement calculation is based on the inflated preretirement expense amount for the retirement year. This will become clearer as we move ahead.

Preretirement Inflation

To determine the effects of inflation between now and retirement, we use the "estimated annual expense" amount, which is $71,400 in the example, and the number of years until retirement. The table below shows the change in the annual expense amount at different rates of inflation and different time periods until retirement. Using the table, if I'm age thirty right now and plan to retire at age sixty-five, then I would use the column for "35 years until retirement." The current inflation rate is about 2 percent, so I would look across the "2%" row, and where they intersect is my inflated expense amount at retirement.

For our example, the estimated annual retirement expenses of $71,400 in today's dollars become $139,992 when adjusting for 2 percent inflation over thirty-five years. This is an increase of $68,592 in annual expenses. We'll come back to this with an example after we look at inflation during retirement.

Inflation Effects on Annual Expenses before Retirement

Inflation Rate	Years until Retirement				
	20	25	30	35	40
0%	$71,400	$71,400	$71,400	$71,400	$71,400
1%	$86,259	$90,659	$95,284	$100,144	$105,252
2%	$104,016	$114,842	$126,795	**$139,992**	$154,563
3%	$125,200	$145,142	$168,259	$195,058	$226,126

Postretirement Inflation

To determine the effect of inflation during retirement, we start with the inflated expense amount at the retirement date, which was $139,992 in the example, and apply inflation for the amount of time that we'll be retired. For this, we'll need to know how long we will probably live. Actuarial tables, life tables, or mortality tables provide life expectancy estimates for various age groups and situations, but age ninety-five is in common use today, so we'll use that age for the estimate. In the example, we plan to retire at age sixty-five, so with a life expectancy of ninety-five, there will be thirty years of retirement life (and retirement expenses). Simply multiplying the inflated retirement expense amount by thirty years would omit inflation during the retirement period.

Expenses at retirement x Years of retirement = Expense total?

$139,992 x 30 = $4,199,760

If we calculate each year of retirement expenses while applying 2 percent inflation and add the amounts for each year together, the total is $5,792,801.85. *Omitting inflation would give us an estimate that is off by more than $1,500,000 for our retirement savings plan.* I repeat this to highlight the significant impact of inflation in the calculations.

Expense total omitting inflation	$4,199,760.00
Expense total applying inflation	$5,792,801.85
Difference	$1,593,041.85

Figure 12.1   Effects of 2% Annual Inflation on Expenses

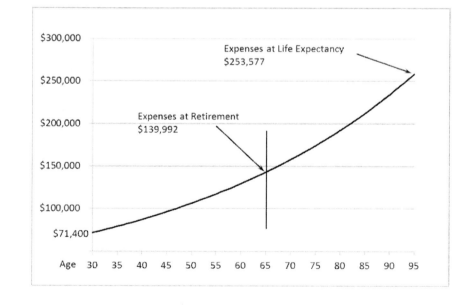

The calculated amounts for the inflation-adjusted expenses are graphed in Figure 12.1 above. The vertical line indicates the example retirement date. Notice that annual expenses of $71,400 grew to $139,992 at retirement, and then to $253,577 at life expectancy.

The total expense amount for the retirement period in the example of $5,792,801.85 is very large, and we'll either have to save an awful lot of money, find a way to lower the expense amount, or earn income in retirement. A pension, social security, or other earnings in retirement will lower the total savings amount needed, but as we'll see later, there are a few other items that we need to take into consideration. In the example, we excluded any interest or return on investment that might be earned during retirement. These would have a positive effect on our situation and will be covered in a later section.

When Retirement Is Near

As our retirement date approaches, we have a much better idea of what our expenses will be for the foreseeable future. Since income will be stopping or significantly reduced, our attention will turn to having adequate cash on hand and to how much we'll be withdrawing from savings to ensure that it lasts. As we get closer to retirement, the calculations that we performed in the previous section become less complicated, and fewer numbers are estimated since we have more information. Whether or not enough has been saved for retirement becomes a major concern, and many people consider setting up a lifetime fixed-income payment through an annuity.

Annuities

Annuities are contracts that can be purchased from life insurance and financial companies that pay us a fixed amount of money for some period of time (in many cases for life). The amount that we're paid is based on the period of time that we will be receiving payments and the purchase price of the annuity. If I'm concerned that I will outlive my retirement savings, I could use my savings (or part of it) to purchase an immediate annuity that will guarantee that I receive a fixed payment for the rest of my life—I can't outlive it.

This sounds like a great plan, but remember that the payment received from the annuity is based on the purchase price. If I haven't saved very much for retirement, then I can't purchase an annuity large enough to provide a fixed income that will cover my expenses. In addition, careful expense estimates need to be made to ensure that there will always be adequate income, and inflation must be considered since we're depending on a fixed amount over a long period of time. If the annuity pays us the amount needed for expenses at retirement, as inflation increases expenses, this amount will not be enough. If the annuity pays us enough to cover the inflated expense amount at life expectancy, then we will need to manage the excess in early years. Either way, the size of the annuity will be based on the purchase price.

There are many varieties of annuities and many provisions within annuities, including continuing payments for spouses if we die, varying the amount paid to us based on market returns, and many other options. There are also cost considerations with annuities, including management fees and a variety of tax considerations. In addition, if we purchase an annuity to provide us with income using most of our retirement savings, then a large portion of our assets is no longer available if we need it.

An annuity can provide fixed income for our lifetime, removing the chance that we will outlive our savings. This might be worth considering, depending on your situation. If you consider an annuity, be sure you have a complete understanding of the annuity and its provisions, and the costs and fees. There are some benefits and some disadvantages as well, so consult an advisor before making a commitment.

Delaying Retirement

To ensure that we will have enough money to cover expenses in retirement, we could decrease monthly expenses, increase income in retirement through part-time employment, or delay our retirement date. Delaying the retirement date eliminates years that we'll be withdrawing from savings to pay expenses, and it adds years that we'll be saving before retirement. In addition, social security and most pension payments are higher if they're started at a later age. The estimates and calculations should be considered for various ages so that we can consider all of the options.

For instance, in the previous example, we calculated thirty years of retirement expenses to be $5,792,801.85. Delaying retirement by five years to age seventy would remove the first 5 years of expenses, and the total expense amount would be $5,049,705.93. We would also have more years to save before we retire.

Total expenses retirement age 65	$5,792,801.85
Total expenses retirement age 70	$5,049,705.93
Difference	$743,095.92

Return-on-Investment in Retirement

Our retirement savings amount will be large, and we haven't yet considered the effects of a return on investment. Even though we'll be withdrawing from savings, a return will be earned either through interest, a return on investment, or a combination of the two. We'll look at this further in the next chapter. The investments will probably be more conservative during retirement to preserve our savings since we'll be withdrawing to pay expenses, so our asset allocation strategy will be changing.

We can't know when the market will turn or for how long, so adjusting our investments ahead of time makes sense. As an example of an asset allocation near the retirement date, a portion of the Vanguard target date fund asset allocations are repeated below. Notice the the changes in allocation over the time period, and the addition of inflation protected bonds beginning at retirement.

Vanguard Target Retirement 2045 Fund (VTIVX) Asset Composition

Asset	-5 Years	Retirement	+5 Years	+10 Years
Cash	0%	0%	4%	5%
Total Bond Market Fund	40%	40%	43%	45%
Inflation Protected Bond Fund	0%	10%	17%	20%
Total International Stock Fund	18%	15%	11%	9%
Total US Stock Market Fund	42%	35%	25%	21%

Source: The Vanguard Group, Inc.

Chapter Summary

Whether retirement is far or near, retirement planning is essential to reviewing all of the factors that affect our retirement savings goal. Obviously, waiting until the day arrives is not a good approach. We should determine an estimated retirement savings amount based on realistic expenses and the effects of inflation, implement a plan to achieve our savings goal, and reevaluate the saving goal as things change. The alternative is being unprepared for a time in our lives when we should have fewer financial responsibilities and should be applying ourselves to more personally fulfilling activities.

Chapter Fourteen

Savings Longevity

The savings longevity calculation determines the length of time that retirement savings will last given an annual withdrawal amount (in dollars or as a percentage), an anticipated return on investment, and an expected inflation rate. Even a slight change to any one of these variables can make a significant difference since the calculations are performed on large amounts of money and cover a very long period of time.

Savings Longevity Methods

There are several ways to calculate savings longevity, and each one makes a different set of assumptions. One method uses a withdrawal rate that is a percentage of the savings; it relies on the return on investment to maintain an adequate retirement balance. Another method uses an annual withdrawal amount that increases as the cost of expenses increase due to inflation. This method assumes that savings is held in conservative assets and is not earning a return on investment. A third is similar to the second, but it includes a return on investment. We'll look at each method to highlight the differences and assumptions and to show how the results differ.

To compare the results of the methods effectively, we'll use the same sample data (shown below). The retirement period will be twenty-five years, the annual inflation rate will be 2 percent, annual expenses at retirement will be $78,000, and the retirement savings starting balance will be $2,500,000.

Savings Longevity Example Data

Retirement period (ages 70–95)	25 years
Annual inflation rate	2%
Annual expenses at retirement	$78,000
Total retirement savings amount	$2,500,000

Method 1:

Withdrawal Amount as a Percentage of the Savings

When we withdraw a percentage of our retirement savings balance each year, and the return-on-investment percentage that we're earning is higher than the withdrawal percentage, our savings should last forever. For example, if the return on investment of my retirement savings is 5 percent, and I'm withdrawing 4 percent of the balance, then I'm earning more from the return each year than I'm withdrawing. The balance actually increases each year as shown below.

Retirement Savings Percentage Withdrawal

Total retirement savings amount	$2,500,000
First year return on investment (5%)	$125,000
First year annual withdrawal (4%)	- $100,000
End of year total retirement savings amount	$2,525,000

This seems like a logical approach at first, but there are a few things that we have to consider if we want to use this method for retirement planning. This approach makes two assumptions. First, it assumes that the amount that we withdraw (4 percent of the savings) is adequate to cover our expenses. In the example, annual expenses were $78,000, so withdrawing 4 percent of $2,500,000 is $100,000 and is sufficient to cover expenses. In fact using this method, any retirement savings amount above $1,950,000 would be able to cover expenses, since

$1,950,000 x 4% = $78,000.

Second, this method assumes that the return on investment will be at least 4 percent in most years (especially the early years of retirement). Unfortunately, we can't forecast future returns. The average annual capital return for the total stock market index was 3.12 percent for the five-year period from 2008 to 2013. This could easily happen again, and in the years when the return is lower than 4 percent, the balance will decrease and our withdrawal amount will then decrease.

In the example, a 4 percent withdrawal from $2,500,000 would be $100,000, which would cover expenses, but we would be taking an additional $22,000 from savings when it isn't necessary.

Retirement Savings 4% Withdrawal

First year withdrawal (4%)	$100,000
First year expenses	$78,000
Excess withdrawal amount	$22,000

As inflation increases the cost of expenses, additional money will be needed, but at the same time, if our retirement savings is earning returns lower than 4 percent, then the withdrawal amount is decreasing the balance. A lower balance will mean a lower withdrawal amount. At some point, the withdrawal amount could decrease to a point when it no longer covers our expenses.

The table below shows ten years of expense, withdrawal, and account balance data for the $2,500,000 retirement savings account. The expense amount column is increasing with 2 percent inflation, the annual withdrawal is 4 percent of the balance, and there is a 3 percent average annual return on investment applied to the savings balance. The withdrawal amount decreases each year as the savings balance decreases, and in the tenth year, the withdrawal amount is lower than the amount needed to cover expenses.

Our expenses would be rising with inflation, but if our savings balance is decreasing, then our withdrawal amount is decreasing. The savings might last, but at some point, the annual withdrawal amount will not be enough to cover our expenses.

Withdrawal Amount as a Percentage of Savings

Age	Year	Annual Expenses 2% Inflation	4% Withdrawal Amount	Account Balance 3% Return
	0			$2,500,000.00
70	1	$78,000.00	$100,000.00	$2,475,000.00
71	2	$79,560.00	$99,000.00	$2,450,250.00
72	3	$81,151.20	$98,010.00	$2,425,747.50
73	4	$82,774.22	$97,029.90	$2,401,490.03
74	5	$84,429.71	$96,059.60	$2,377,475.12
75	6	$86,118.30	$95,099.00	$2,353,700.37
76	7	$87,840.67	$94,148.01	$2,330,163.37
77	8	$89,597.48	$93,206.53	$2,306,861.74
78	9	$91,389.43	$92,274.47	$2,283,793.12
79	10	$93,217.22	$91,351.72	$2,260,955.19

Year 10 withdrawal amount	$91,351.72
Year 10 annual expenses	$93,217.22
Difference	-$1,865.50

Method 2:

Withdrawal Amount Based on Inflation-Adjusted Expenses

This approach to savings longevity increases the withdrawal amount with the inflation rate to compensate for increases in expenses. We start with the total amount of savings and subtract the inflation-adjusted annual expense amount each year from the balance. This method assumes that the retirement savings amount would be kept in an insured savings account (earning very little interest), so return on investment is not included.

The first and last three years of data for the example are shown below. The annual withdrawal amount increases each year with inflation, and the balance in the account is reduced. As long as the inflation rate remains at 2 percent or below, the savings will last through the retirement period.

Annual Withdrawal Amount Increased with 2% Inflation

Age	Year	Annual Withdrawal	Account Balance
	0		$2,500,000.00
70	1	$78,000.00	$2,422,000.00
71	2	$79,560.00	$2,342,440.00
72	3	$81,151.20	$2,261,288.80
⋮	⋮	⋮	⋮
92	23	$120,586.41	$250,092.87
93	24	$122,998.14	$127,094.73
94	25	$125,458.11	$1,636.62

With this method, if we need to withdraw more in some years to pay expenses, then our savings will run out sooner than expected. But this method does not consider a return on investment, and even a small return will have a significant effect on the balance because of the large amount in savings. The table below shows the return on investment for

$2,500,000 in the first year of retirement at different rates of return. This could be a large amount to overlook.

Return on Investment during the First Year of Retirement

Rate of Return on Investment	First-Year Return on Investment
1%	$25,000
2%	$50,000
3%	$75,000
4%	$100,000
5%	$125,000

Method 3:

Withdrawal Amount Based on Inflation-Adjusted Expenses and Including Return on Investment

The table on the previous page showed the results of withdrawing an inflation-adjusted amount each year with no return on investment, and the retirement savings balance lasted exactly twenty-five years. The table below shows the number of years that the sample savings amount will last when we withdraw the inflation-adjusted amount but include different rates of return that the savings would be earning.

Savings Longevity for $2,500,000, with Return on Investment

Rate of Return on Investment	Savings Longevity
1%	28 years
2%	32 years
3%	39 years
4%	51 years

The table above shows that with a 4 percent return, $2,500,000 in retirement savings will last twice as long as needed. This shows that if we'll be earning a reasonable return on investment, our retirement savings goal could be smaller than $2,500,000 and still provide for expenses through the retirement period.

Let's review the details of the first few years of retirement data. In the first year (shown below), $78,000 is withdrawn, but savings only decreases by $28,000 because of the return on investment.

First Year of Retirement

Starting savings balance in retirement	$2,500,000
Return on investment (2%)	+$50,000
Annual withdrawal	-$78,000
Ending balance	$2,472,000

$2,500,000 - $2,472,000 = $28,000 (change in balance)

In the second year of retirement (shown below), the expense amount increases because of inflation, and the return on investment decreases slightly since the total savings balance is slightly lower. In the second year, the balance only decreases by $30,120 due to the return on investment. This continues through the retirement period, and after thirty-two years (not twenty-five years), the balance in this example is finally depleted.

Second Year of Retirement

Retirement savings balance	$2,472,000
Return on investment (2%)	+$49,440
Annual withdrawal	-$79,560
Ending balance	$2,441,880

$2,472,000 - $2,441,880 = $30,120 (change in balance)

Many people count on a 6 or 7 percent return on investment in their retirement years, since these percentages could be considered long-term averages for market returns. We need to remember that long-term averages include downturns in the market. Counting on a high return in retirement could put us in a bad position, especially in the early years when the impact of low or negative returns is even greater due to the large savings amount being affected.

As an example, let's say that we're in the first year of retirement, and we're counting on a 7 percent return on investment. If the actual return on investment is 2 percent, this would be $125,000 less than we expected to earn (shown below), and could have a major impact on our retirement plans. It's better to be conservative when making these estimates.

One-Year Hypothetical Return on Investment $2,500,000

Actual Return 2%	$50,000
Planned Return 7%	$175,000
Difference	-$125,000

The Right Savings Amount

Our retirement savings goal amount will depend on the method we use for estimating and on the assumptions that we make in the calculations. If the actual return on investment is higher than our assumption or the rate of inflation is lower than our assumption, it could add many years to savings longevity. Of course, the opposite could happen as well.

The prudent approach is to estimate the expenses for the retirement year as we did in the beginning of this chapter. Then apply an expected inflation rate for each year of the retirement period and add them together to determine the total retirement period expense amount. This total amount could then be used as the retirement savings goal. A cautious return-on-investment percentage can be applied to the savings amount to determine how long savings will last, and then if needed, we can adjust the total retirement savings amount. We adjust the plan and savings goal amount based on an expected rate of return.

To review the final step of adjusting the goal, we'll use the same sample data and calculate the complete savings longevity schedule. To be consistent, the initial withdrawal amount will be $78,000, and we'll apply a 2 percent inflation adjustment each year. We'll also assume a 4 percent average annual return on investment.

Savings Longevity Example Data

Retirement period (ages 70–95)	25 years
Annual expenses at retirement	$78,000
Annual inflation rate	2%
Average annual return on investment	4%

In the complete schedule of calculations in the table below, the savings balance increases at first due to the return on investment, and the withdrawal (expense) amount increases due to inflation. In the nineteenth year, the withdrawal amount becomes larger than the return and the savings balance begins to decrease. But at the end of the twenty-five year period, the retirement savings is still larger than the starting balance.

This means that with a 4 percent annual return on investment and 2 percent inflation, the retirement savings amount could actually be lower than $2,500,000 and still provide for expenses and last through the retirement period.

Savings Longevity Analysis - $2,500,000

Age	Year	Annual Withdrawal	Return on Investment	Account Balance
70	1	$78,000.00	$100,000.00	$2,522,000.00
71	2	$79,560.00	$100,880.00	$2,543,320.00
72	3	$81,151.20	$101,732.80	$2,563,901.60
73	4	$82,774.22	$102,556.06	$2,583,683.44
74	5	$84,429.71	$103,347.34	$2,602,601.07
75	6	$86,118.30	$104,104.04	$2,620,586.81
76	7	$87,840.67	$104,823.47	$2,637,569.61
77	8	$89,597.48	$105,502.78	$2,653,474.92
78	9	$91,389.43	$106,139.00	$2,668,224.48
79	10	$93,217.22	$106,728.98	$2,681,736.24
80	11	$95,081.56	$107,269.45	$2,693,924.12
81	12	$96,983.20	$107,756.96	$2,704,697.89
82	13	$98,922.86	$108,187.92	$2,713,962.95
83	14	$100,901.32	$108,558.52	$2,721,620.15
84	15	$102,919.34	$108,864.81	$2,727,565.61
85	16	$104,977.73	$109,102.62	$2,731,690.51
86	17	$107,077.28	$109,267.62	$2,733,880.84
87	18	$109,218.83	$109,355.23	$2,734,017.24
88	**19**	**$111,403.21**	**$109,360.69**	**$2,731,974.73**
89	20	$113,631.27	$109,278.99	$2,727,622.44
90	21	$115,903.90	$109,104.90	$2,720,823.44
91	22	$118,221.97	$108,832.94	$2,711,434.41
92	23	$120,586.41	$108,457.38	$2,699,305.37
93	24	$122,998.14	$107,972.21	$2,684,279.44
94	25	$125,458.11	$107,371.18	$2,666,192.51

We can lower the total savings amount and recalculate the table and eventually determine an amount that will comfortably last through the retirement period. This would lower the total amount that we need to save for retirement.

In the recalculated schedule below, the retirement savings amount has been changed to $1,500,000, and it lasts through the retirement period.

Savings Longevity Analysis - $1,500,000

Age	Year	Annual Withdrawal	Return on Investment	Account Balance
70	1	$78,000.00	$60,000.00	$1,482,000.00
71	2	$79,560.00	$59,280.00	$1,461,720.00
72	3	$81,151.20	$58,468.80	$1,439,037.60
73	4	$82,774.22	$57,561.50	$1,413,824.88
74	5	$84,429.71	$56,553.00	$1,385,948.17
75	6	$86,118.30	$55,437.93	$1,355,267.79
76	7	$87,840.67	$54,210.71	$1,321,637.83
77	8	$89,597.48	$52,865.51	$1,284,905.86
78	9	$91,389.43	$51,396.23	$1,244,912.67
79	10	$93,217.22	$49,796.51	$1,201,491.95
80	11	$95,081.56	$48,059.68	$1,154,470.07
81	12	$96,983.20	$46,178.80	$1,103,665.67
82	13	$98,922.86	$44,146.63	$1,048,889.44
83	14	$100,901.32	$41,955.58	$989,943.70
84	15	$102,919.34	$39,597.75	$926,622.11
85	16	$104,977.73	$37,064.88	$858,709.26
86	17	$107,077.28	$34,348.37	$785,980.35
87	18	$109,218.83	$31,439.21	$708,200.73
88	19	$111,403.21	$28,328.03	$625,125.55
89	20	$113,631.27	$25,005.02	$536,499.30
90	21	$115,903.90	$21,459.97	$442,055.38
91	22	$118,221.97	$17,682.22	$341,515.62
92	23	$120,586.41	$13,660.62	$234,589.83
93	24	$122,998.14	$9,383.59	$120,975.28
94	25	$125,458.11	$4,839.01	$356.18

Unless there are a number of years with very poor returns or the inflation rate increases above 2 percent, $1.5 million would be an adequate savings amount for this example. This is $1 million less than we originally planned, and it shows the benefits of analyzing savings longevity using different methods and assumptions. The steps are repeated below for convenience.

Determining Retirement Savings Goal

- Estimate expenses for the retirement year.
- Apply inflation to expenses over the retirement period.
- Determine the total retirement expense amount.
- Apply a conservative return on investment to the savings.
- Calculate savings longevity.
- Adjust the total savings amount if needed and recalculate.

Once retirement begins, we should review the amounts annually. If the return on investment or inflation rate changes, recalculating the amounts from that date forward will show if we need to adjust our plans.

Chapter Summary

There are some popular rules of thumb for establishing retirement savings goals and determining savings longevity, but when we perform the analysis ourselves and include our own financial information, we have more confidence in the results. We know that we've accounted for inflation and a reasonable return on investment based on our plans for asset allocation in retirement. When our situation changes, we can reevaluate savings longevity based on new information and adjust our plans to ensure that we have the right savings goal to support us through life expectancy.

Chapter Fifteen

Taxes

Tax laws change every year to some degree, but there are a few general principles that we can follow that will make tax time less of a burden. The first has to do with tax-related information. Regardless of how we file our taxes, all of our tax-related documents should be placed in a separate folder or envelope throughout the year. This includes medical expense and charitable donation receipts, as well as employer, bank, and financial statements. Things are bound to be lost or forgotten over the course of the year, so keeping everything together at least guarantees that we'll have it when tax season rolls around.

It's also a good idea to separate the expense documents in the folder by category (medical, charity, etc.) and use a spread sheet or software to track the expenses as they occur. The list should include the date of the expense and how it was paid (check number, credit card, etc.). This additional information will make filing income tax forms much faster and easier.

The IRS (Internal Revenue Service) allows us to take a standard deduction for income tax, but many people find that their tax burden is lower by itemizing deductions using the Schedule A and filing the long 1040 tax form. Itemized deductions include some medical care, charitable contributions, some interest payments, and some taxes including property taxes. If you complete and file your own tax forms (which I don't recommend), you should complete the forms both ways to see which way of filing is more beneficial for you. Of course, if you don't keep track of charitable contributions and medical expenses, then there's no way of knowing if you can benefit from the deductions, because there are various thresholds to consider.

For instance, if medical expenses must be more than 7.5 percent of our adjusted gross income before they can be deducted and my adjusted gross income is $50,000, then only my medical expenses above $3,750 can be deducted. If my medical expenses for the year were $5,600, then $1,850 could be deducted as shown below.

Threshold for deduction: $50,000 x 7.5% = $3,750

Expenses minus threshold: $5,600 - $3,750 = $1,850

This is one example, but there are many deductions that have thresholds or limits like charitable contributions, state and local taxes, miscellaneous deductions, work-related expenses, and others. An employer will keep track of the items that appear on the W-2 form that we get in February like wages and withholdings, but we need to keep track of the rest. If we don't keep track of expenses throughout the year, we can't complete the calculation and take advantage of the deduction.

Federal Withholding

Employers withhold various taxes from our pay checks throughout the year, and when we file our tax forms, the amount that was withheld is compared to the income taxes that we owe. If the amount withheld is too small, then we will need to make a payment for the difference. If more than enough was withheld, then we receive a tax refund or return. The amount withheld is based on information on the W-4 form that we filed with our employer when we were hired. If we're receiving a large check from the IRS each year, then our federal income tax withholding amount might be too high.

The amount withheld from our pay should be slightly higher than the amount of income tax we'll actually pay. If a large amount is being withheld, then we're just using the government as a savings account that earns no interest and then getting a big tax refund check each year. It's nice to get a large check each spring, but we're giving up the opportunity to use the money that's being withheld throughout the year. As an example, if I receive an income tax refund of $10,400, then my weekly federal withholding amount is about $200 higher each week than it really needs to be to cover my taxes.

$200 x 52 weeks = $10,400

If I can lower the withholding amount by $100 each week, it would still provide an adequate tax cushion, and at the same time, it would increase my take-home pay. Instead of having the government hold this money throughout the year, I could use it to pay off debt (which is costing me interest) or have it directly deposited to a savings or investment account each week, which would earn interest.

To change the amount withheld requires an adjustment to the W-4 form held by our employer. If you're in this situation, add this topic to the list of questions to ask your accountant at tax time, because adjusting the withholding amount must be done carefully. If we make the withholding amount too low, we'll be writing a check to the government at tax time, and in some cases there could be an underpayment penalty. It's better to have a little too much withheld than not enough.

If we're self-employed, then we should be making periodic tax payments throughout the year. An accountant can determine the right amount to ensure that we don't incur penalties.

Homeowner Benefits

Owning a home with a mortgage provides some income tax benefit since mortgage interest is tax deductible, but we need to understand that the amount we pay in interest is much larger than the amount of the tax benefit. Many people think that the full amount of mortgage interest that they pay is subtracted from their income taxes, but mortgage interest is a deduction, not a subtraction. Deductions lower (or modify) our taxable income amount, which in turn lowers our tax payment. So the tax benefit from mortgage interest is a percentage of the full amount of mortgage interest that we pay.

The percentage of the tax benefit is based on our tax bracket, and our tax bracket is determined by our taxable income. Most of our tax deductions are handled this way, so the impact of taxes in personal finance is well worth considering. We'll walk through an example to show how this is calculated. As a point of reference, the tax brackets for 2012 based on taxable income for single individuals and those filing married joint returns are listed below. A large majority of Americans are in the 25 percent bracket.

2012 Tax Brackets Based on Taxable Income

Single Taxable Income (between)		Bracket	Married Filing Joint Taxable Income (between)		Bracket
$0	$8,700	10%	$0	$17,400	10%
$8,700	$35,350	15%	$17,400	$70,700	15%
$35,350	$86,650	25%	$70,700	$142,700	25%
$86,650	$178,650	28%	$142,700	$217,450	28%
$178,650	$388,350	33%	$217,450	$388,350	33%
$388,350	and above	35%	$388,350	and above	35%

Data Source: US Internal Revenue Service

If we're single and have $86,000 in taxable income, we would be in the 25 percent tax bracket, and our tax benefit from mortgage interest would be just $0.25 for each dollar of mortgage interest paid. To show the details of this example in dollars, we'll calculate the tax with and without the deduction.

Without the deduction, we would pay $21,500 in income tax, which is 25 percent of the $86,000 in taxable income (shown below).

Income Tax Based on Taxable Income

Taxable income x Tax bracket = Income tax

$86,000 x 25% = $21,500

If our mortgage interest paid for the year is $8,299, then that amount is subtracted from our taxable income (not from our taxes). The new taxable income amount is then used to determine the amount of taxes that we will pay. The new or adjusted income amount will be lower, and therefore our taxes will be lower.

Income Tax Based on Adjusted Taxable Income

Taxable income - Mortgage interest = Adjusted taxable income

$86,000 - $8,299 = $77,701

Adjusted taxable income x Tax bracket = Income tax

$77,701.00 x 25% = $19,425.25

Mortgage Interest Deduction Benefits

Income tax without the deduction	$21,500.00
Income tax with the mortgage interest deduction	$19,425.25
Benefit of mortgage interest deduction	$2,074.75

Without the deduction, income taxes are $21,500, and with the deduction, they are $19,425.25. The difference in taxes paid as a result of the mortgage interest deduction is $2,074.75, even though we paid $8,299 in mortgage interest.

Keep this in mind if you're considering paying down or paying off your mortgage. You'll lose the deduction, but the benefits from mortgage interest are not as large as we might think. In addition, Congress frequently considers limiting or eliminating this tax deduction, so keep an eye out for changes or check with a tax professional.

Property taxes work the same way. The property tax deduction lowers (or adjusts) our income, which is then used to determine the income tax amount. If we continue with the example above and assume annual property taxes are $9,000 and subtract the mortgage interest and property taxes together, the taxable income amount is lowered to $68,701 (which is still within the 25 percent tax bracket).

Income Tax Based on Adjusted Taxable Income

Mortgage Interest and Property Taxes

Taxable income	$86,000
Mortgage interest	-$8,299
Property taxes	-$9,000
Adjusted taxable income	$68,701

Adjusted taxable income x Tax bracket = Income tax

$68,701.00 x 25% = $17,175.25

The change in income tax as a result of the property tax deduction is an additional $2,250 although property taxes paid were $9,000. The amount paid in mortgage interest and property taxes together total

$17,299, and the tax benefit (shown below) is $4,324.75. This is 25 percent of the amount paid (or $0.25 returned for each dollar spent).

Mortgage Interest and Property Tax Deduction Benefits

Mortgage interest paid	$8,299
Property taxes paid	$9,000
Total	$17,299
Taxable income without deductions	$86,000
Taxable income with deductions	$68,701
Income tax without deductions	$21,500.00
Income tax with deductions	$17,175.25
Tax benefit from deductions	$4,324.75

Earnings and Interest

For savings and investments, an IRA is the most tax-efficient way to save for the future. As mentioned earlier, there are several types of IRAs, and due to frequent changes in tax laws, consult the latest IRA information, an accountant, or a financial advisor, especially if you're considering an IRA for the first time. Although taxes on investments tend to have the greatest effect on people in the highest tax brackets, understanding investment taxation can help us to keep more of our earnings. There is a maximum annual amount that we can deposit to an IRA, and if you're already saving that amount, then consider some tax-friendly investments like tax-advantage mutual funds.

If possible, investments with larger tax impacts should be kept within an IRA account where taxes are deferred. For instance, many investments incur capital gains and capital losses, which are the differences between the net purchase price and net sale price of an investment. Funds that buy and sell stocks incur these gains and losses, which are passed on to the investor. Recall from the chapter on mutual funds that actively managed funds have a lot of buying and selling of assets (turnover ratio), so the tax impact can be significant. Mutual fund companies typically provide tax-related information on their websites for their funds including returns before and after taxes.

Tax laws may change in this area as well, so consult the latest information, an accountant, or a financial advisor to determine the tax impact in your situation. When you receive tax forms for your investments, read them and gain an understanding of the tax implications of your current investments. Also be sure to keep these forms in your tax file together with the quarterly statements that you receive, because you'll need them at tax time.

Tax Professionals

Income tax laws change almost every year, and we shouldn't assume that we have the latest information or that we know how it could apply to our tax situation. Federal and state income tax planning and filing are very complex, and we can overlook important details and considerations. The best solution is to rely on a certified public accountant (CPA) who will have up-to-date knowledge about current and pending tax laws and how they apply to our circumstances. CPAs don't just do our taxes, they provide expert tax-related financial advice and guidance, and they're available for questions all year long.

If we do our own income tax forms by hand or use software products, we're limited by what we know about tax laws and what we can determine from the software instructions. With a professional, we can ask questions and find out how changes in our lives, income, or expenses might affect our tax situation in the coming years.

If you're not completely familiar with the tax implications of any of the areas listed below, seriously consider finding and building a relationship with a good certified public accountant.

Typical Areas that Affect Income Tax

- standard deductions and personal exemptions
- alternative minimum tax (AMT)
- IRAs and 401(k) plans and qualified plan contributions
- estate and gift tax limits
- required minimum distributions (RMD)
- child tax credit
- charitable donations
- itemized deduction phase-outs
- sales tax deductions
- tax-exempt interest reporting
- health savings accounts
- education savings accounts
- taxable versus tax-deferred accounts

State Taxes

I've heard and read a lot about tax-friendly states and the differences in property, income, and sales taxes in different areas. I did some research and state-to-state comparisons, and I found that many states with low property taxes make up for it with higher sales or income taxes and vice versa. There are also many counties that add taxes of their own. Some states don't tax social security, but they tax interest and investment income, and others tax certain portions of retirement earnings. If you're considering relocation, be sure to use current information and to tally up all of the state and county income, property, and sales taxes for comparison. You'll be surprised at how similar the tax situations are between states when you compare the complete tax pictures.

Chapter Summary

Taxes affect our personal finances in many ways, and having a basic awareness can help us make tax-efficient decisions without a lot of calculations. Simply keeping all tax-related documents together and tracking deductible amounts will make life easier at tax time, and seeking professional tax advice will ensure that we're applying up-to-date information to our financial situation including the tax withholding amount from our pay, the tax benefits of homeownership, and the effects of taxes on our choice of investments.

Chapter Sixteen

Conclusion

Our personal finance goal is financial independence, which means that we have spending under control, debt eliminated, savings established and growing, and a well-thought-out lifelong financial plan that includes caring for our survivors. It takes some work and it takes time, but don't lose heart. If it were easy, everyone would be financially independent. Just take one step at a time: establish a plan, stick to the plan, and review and update the plan as things change. Track your progress, and as the situation improves and financial independence becomes a real possibility, you'll be glad for every minute that you spent and every dollar that you saved. Let's review some key points.

- Establish a budget.
- Get spending under control.
- Eliminate debt.
- Develop a saving plan.
- Prepare for survivors.
- Plan for the transition to retirement.
- Invest wisely.
- Reduce the tax burden.
- Take the time to manage finances.

Establish a Budget

We can't manage our money without a budget, and we can't form a plan to make our financial situation better unless we know and review the details of our financial condition. Creating a budget that faces reality and uses facts tells us exactly where we're spending and how much. It will also expose opportunities for trimming expenses and identifying any discretionary income that could be put to good use eliminating debt or increasing savings. Establishing and managing from a budget is the part of personal finance that most people would prefer to overlook, but it's also the most valuable.

Get Spending under Control

Once we have a budget, it will be easy to see where we might need more discipline in our spending. We live in an economy based on consumption, and we're constantly bombarded with ads that want to separate us from our money. It's difficult to continually screen what we see and hear and to remind ourselves that being able to buy something isn't the same as being able to afford it. We need to continually make this important distinction. Living within or below our means is the only way we can break the debt cycle and that means controlling where the money is going. Being a wise consumer isn't about being cheap. It's about being practical and taking care of needs first and wants second.

Eliminate Debt

With a working budget and spending under control, we can begin to reduce and eventually eliminate debt. Whether we tackle the largest debt, smallest debt, or highest-interest debt first, we need to form a workable debt-elimination plan focused on the debt that will provide the greatest benefit and that allows us to keep track of our progress.

Seeing the balances decrease each month and seeing how much we're no longer paying in interest is a great encouragement to keep going.

Develop a Saving Plan

Saving doesn't have to wait until everything else is taken care of; in fact, if we wait until then we may never start. We have to develop a saving plan, carve a few dollars out of our income and start saving for the future. We need some accessible savings for the unexpected, an emergency fund to cover expenses for a few months just in case and a large, long-term savings amount for later in life. The hardest parts about saving are getting started and leaving it alone so that compound interest can work in our favor. If we know how much we need to save and why, we have a greater incentive to save. Form a short-term and long-term plan including the saving amount goals and keep track of your progress. You'll be surprised by how quickly it grows.

Prepare for Survivors

If we have a spouse or dependents, we need to consider and prepare for their financial situation in case we suddenly pass away. There will be expenses before and after retirement age, our debts will need to be paid, and there may be additional planned expenses like a college fund for children. The effects of inflation should also be accounted for in the calculations. After determining the full amount that would be needed, a review of savings and life insurance will show whether or not we need to make an adjustment. Since these figures change, we should review the information at least once every year. We don't know what tomorrow will bring, but we can prepare and provide lifelong financial protection for our loved ones … just in case.

Plan for the Transition to Retirement

At some point in the future, there will be a change to our work life. Retirement age will arrive, and we will experience a major transition. We can prepare ahead of time by determining retirement expenses, potential income, the amount we'll need in savings, and how long we'll need our savings to last. Then we can apply this information to our long-term saving plan to ensure that we'll have what we need in retirement. We should also review and update this information every year or whenever there's a change in our financial situation. Waiting until later to plan for retirement just adds to the problem. The sooner we get started, the easier it will be.

Invest Wisely

Prudent investing requires a little homework and analysis to determine the asset allocation strategy that fits our needs and our tolerance for risk. Our asset allocation should be diverse to dampen market volatility, incorporate the risk-return relationship of a mix of stocks and bonds, take advantage of the lower costs of index mutual funds, and stay clear of high management and other fees that reduce our returns. We should only invest at our comfort level, and never invest in something that we don't fully understand. Once our portfolio is established, we should monitor our returns and asset allocation to ensure that our portfolio performance is in line with our expectations and our risk preferences.

Reduce the Tax Burden

Since we file our taxes annually, during the year we don't think about things that affect our tax situation—but we should. Keeping tax-related documents together and tracking deductible expenses throughout the year will make tax time less of a burden. In addition, our withholding allowance, investments, and filing status should be reviewed regularly to be sure we're not overlooking a financial opportunity. A certified public accountant would be aware of any tax laws that apply to our situation and can provide invaluable guidance for the future.

Take the Time to Manage Finances

It takes time to manage personal finances. It's just that simple. If we don't take the time to manage things, then they will eventually manage us. If you're just getting started, it may take a few hours each week to update and review your whole financial picture. Once your plans are established and you become more familiar with your financial situation, it takes less time to maintain the data and update plans. Reviewing the information and seeing the progress we're making is also very rewarding and well worth the effort. We can't leave our personal finances to chance—it just doesn't work that way.

Where We Go from Here

It might seem as if we've covered a lot of material in this book, but these are the basics that everyone should know about the areas of personal finance. The goal is financial independence, and by applying the information we've reviewed, we're better equipped to make the right financial decisions to achieve that goal. We just need to get started and stick with it. To help, I've included a list of books for further reading since there's always more to learn, and this is a vitally important part of our lives. Financial independence is an achievable goal.

Further Reading

Bogle, John C. *The Clash of the Cultures: Investment vs. Speculation.* Hoboken, NJ: John Wiley & Sons, 2012.

Bogle, John C. *Enough: True Measures of Money, Business, and Life.* Hoboken, NJ: John Wiley & Sons, 2009.

Ellis, Charles D. *Winning the Loser's Game: Timeless Strategies for Successful Investing.* New York: McGraw-Hill, 2009.

MalKiel, Burton G. *A Random Walk Down Wall Street: The Time-Tested Strategy for Successful Investing* (10th Ed.). New York: Norton, W. W. & Company, 2011.

Merriman, Paul A. *Live It Up Without Outliving Your Money: Getting the Most From Your Investments in Retirement.* Hoboken, NJ: John Wiley & Sons, 2008.

Stanley, Thomas J., and William D. Danko. *The Millionaire Next Door: The Surprising Secrets of America's Wealthy.* New York: Pocket Books, 1996.

Resources

AnnualCreditReport.com—obtain a free credit report once each year

BankRate.com—interest rate information and calculators

InvestingInBonds.com—everything about bonds; hosted by the Securities Industry and Financial Markets Association (SIFMA)

Jazersolutions.com—personal finance software

MFEA.com—Mutual Fund Education Alliance; nonprofit mutual fund information

MorningStar.com—stock and fund information

SSA.gov—Social Security Administration information and estimates

Treasury.gov and TreasuryDirect.gov—U S Department of Treasury; bond and security rates and purchasing information

Vanguard.com—the Vanguard Group website

Let Jazer 100 do the Math for You.

Jazer 100—Personal Version is for home use by individuals who want to manage their personal finances. This multiwindow program simplifies comprehensive financial information review, analysis, planning, tracking, what-if scenarios, and forecasting in an integrated and easy-to-use tool. Many values are shared automatically among the various sections to simplify data entry, increase visibility, and ensure accuracy.

Jazer 200—Academic Version is designed as an aid to teaching, understanding, learning, and applying comprehensive financial management knowledge. The program is designed in a building-block format and includes a sample data file that coincides with User Manual examples to shorten the learning curve and accelerate the learning process. Students can use the comprehensive planning and analysis segments for assignments, their own personal information, what-if excursions, and investigating the impacts of various financial conditions and decisions. Scenarios are provided as an aid to course development and instruction.

Jazer 300—Professional Version is designed for financial professionals. This provides client review, analysis, planning, and forecasting capabilities in an integrated multiwindow program and includes an information-gathering worksheet and client report generation. The program segments share information and build a complete client package through integrated calculations and data handling, to automate and simplify data input.

continued on back

Jazer Program Capabilities and Segments

- ✓ Budget Determination and Analysis, and Balance Sheet
- ✓ Debt Elimination Planning and Tracking
- ✓ Mortgage Tracking and Analysis, and Loan Tracking (4 sections)
- ✓ Monthly Financial Manager
- ✓ Savings Performance Tracking and Details
- ✓ Investment Tracking, Details, and Asset Allocation
- ✓ Investment and Savings Forecasts
- ✓ Primary and Benchmark Portfolios
- ✓ Retirement Planning, Retirement Expenses, and Savings Longevity
- ✓ Economic Value and Survivorship Planning
- ✓ Advanced Calculators and Display Options
- ✓ Tax Journal and Personal Note Pad

Simplicity: The various segments of the program share information and build a complete personal finance package through integrated calculations and data handling. This automates and simplifies much of the data input. In addition, a sample data file is provided that coincides with the User Manual to explain each section.

Security: Personal data is secure and under full owner control with encoded data files and password protection capabilities, coupled with a stand-alone design that does not transmit or receive personal information across the Internet.

Accuracy: The equations used for calculations are industry standard financial equations utilizing a very high level of precision, extensive testing, and results comparisons to ensure accuracy.

For more information, visit www.jazersolutions.com

CPSIA information can be obtained at www.ICGtesting.com
Printed in the USA
LVOW06*1552140714

394266LV00002B/22/P

9 781491 705223